TO Bob Melge
with
all my best.

Pieracci and Shelley
An Italian *Ur-Cenci*

𝔖cripta 𝔥umanistica

Directed by
BRUNO M. DAMIANI
The Catholic University of America

ADVISORY BOARD

Pieracci and Shelley
An Italian *Ur-Cenci*

George Yost

Scripta humanistica

19

Library of Congress Cataloging-in-Publication Data

Yost, George, 1910–
    Pieracci and Shelley, an Italian ur-Cenci.

    (Scripta humanistica ; 19)
    Includes the original Italian and English
translation version of Vincenzo Pieracci's Beatrice
Cenci.
    Includes bibliographies.
    1. Shelley, Percy Bysshe, 1792–1822. Cenci--Sources.
2. Pieracci, Vincenzo, 1768–1834. Beatrice Cenci.
3. Shelley, Percy Bysshe, 1792–1822--Knowledge--Italy.
4. Pieracci, Vincenzo, 1768–1834--Influence--Shelley.
5. Cenci, Beatrice, 1577–1599, in fiction, drama,
poetry, etc. 6. Cenci, Beatrice, 1577–1599--Drama.
7. Italy in literature. I. Pieracci, Vincenzo, 1768–1834.
Beatrice Cenci. English & Italian. 1986. II. Title.
III. Series.
PR5408.Y67 1986   822'.7   86–70334
ISBN 0-916379-33-7

Library of Congress Catalog Card Number: 86-070334
International Standard Book Number: 0-916379-33-7

Publisher and Distributor:
SCRIPTA HUMANISTICA
1383 Kersey Lane
Potomac, Maryland 20854 U.S.A.

Contents

Preface

My reasons for doing this work are twofold. First, in spite of the fact that Shelley has been much written about, this study offers new insights into Shelley, in particular his mind, his working methods, and his materials. His use of the first play to appear on the old historical murder, the now-forgotten play, *Beatrice Cenci*, by Vincenzio Pieracci, which preceded Shelley's play, *The Cenci*, by three years, supplies the material basis.

The differences between a classical play by an Italian dramatist and Shelley's romantic and Shakespearean play are many, and these are treated first. Next are the positive connections, which include an important character similar in name and function in both plays, who appears nowhere else before Pieracci, whether in history or the legendary prose account available to Shelley. Last is a considerable number of parallels which may or may not reflect Shelley's use of Pieracci. Shelley characteristically reshaped his materials with such a free hand that it is difficult to be certain.

Included in a footnote as corroborating evidence on Shelley's methods of working with his materials are a bibliography and a summary from many writers of Shelley's use of Shakespeare, particularly in *The Cenci*.

My second reason for doing this work is to add one more

accessible version of the historical and legendary Cenci story to the distinguished list of poems, novels, and plays on the subject that includes, among many, the fiction of Stendhal (*The Cenci*), Francesco Domenico Guerrazi (*Beatrice Cenci*), Alexandre Dumas père (*The Cenci*), Agostino Ademollo (*Beatrice Cenci Roman*), and Frederick Proskosch (*A Tale for Midnight*); as well as the dramas of Shelley, G. B. Niccolini (*Beatrice Cenci*), Astolphe de Custine (*Beatrix Cenci*), Juliusz Slowacki (*Beatrix Cenci*), Antonin Artaud (*The Cenci*), Umberto Liberatore (*Beatrice Cenci*), and Alberto Moravia (*Beatrice Cenci*).

As part of the effort to resurrect Pieracci's play from a limbo of about one hundred and seventy years, the work includes my translation, with assistance, of the Italian play and the Italian play itself. I am aware that it is difficult to do justice in a translation to the letter and spirit of the original, and a translator must be on guard lest he "make the Book [his] own," as Andrew Marvell has warned, or so translate as to prove some thesis or other. The Italians have an expression, *traduttore traditore* (a translator is a betrayer), and there are equivalent expressions in other cultures. The great scholar Benjamin Jowett has been said to have translated Plato into membership in the Church of England. If, as is possible, Shelley himself translated the manuscript Es that is his principal source, he too has not escaped criticism. But here the criticism is on the other side, on grounds of awkwardness. A great French critic's observation covers both sides. A translation is like a woman: if it is beautiful, it is unfaithful; if it is faithful, it is ugly. For reasons that will be obvious, I have elected in this translation to err if I must on the side of literal accuracy. In any event, the presence in this book of the English and the Italian will allow the reader to check for himself.

In the text of the first section the reader will find summaries of the plot of Pieracci's play; of Shelley's main source, "Relation of the Death of the Family of the Cenci" (Es); and of Shelley's play. Other materials appearing in footnotes and new to scholarship are the way in which Shelley probably first became acquainted with Pieracci's play; a life of Pieracci; a contemporary review of the *Beatrice Cenci* and other plays in the 1816 volume; listings of other volumes and plays of Pieracci; materials from Pieracci's prefaces, including his theory of tragedy; the persistence of interest in the Cenci story; why the Cenci story, now so popular in drama, was slow to receive its first, the Pieraccian, treatment; and conjectures why Pieracci, who published some eighteen plays, has escaped fame, is not mentioned in the great, many-volumed, biographically oriented *Enciclopedia Italiana*.

I wish to acknowledge my indebtedness to Professors Claude Flory and Harold C. Gross for bringing the Pieracci play out of limbo and to my attention; to the Cornell University Library for supplying me with a text of the play; and to Associate Professor Richard Hilary and Professor Azzurra Givens of the Modern Language Department of Florida State University for their checking my translation of the Italian. The latter have saved me from many a mistake and have also helped me in my investigation of Italian background. I am also indebted to Professor Duane Meeter of the Statistics Department of Florida State University for the method of probability applied in the footnote on the character of Camillo. The Florida State University Foundation has also awarded me two grants that have assisted in the preparation of the manuscript. Doctor Sylvana Palmerio of the *Enciclopedia Italiana*, Rome, in an extended correspondence has been generous with her time and expertise in finding me reviews and various leads in the drawn-out process of tracking down the elusive Pieracci. Charles Miller, Lucille Higgs, Phyllis Holzenberg, Louise Clay, Joseph Evans, James Myers, and others of the Florida State University Library staff have been very helpful over the years. During my recent study at the British Museum Library, Theresa Pickering, Chris Michaelides, Edwina Open, and Ronald Browne of the staff assisted in my researches in books and other materials. Mrs. Muriel Stewart and Mrs. Daphne Liedy have patiently and skillfully typed the much-revised manuscript. I must in conclusion thank my wife Ruth for her kind support in these efforts.

G. Y.

Florida State University
May 1, 1985

PART I

An Italian *Ur-Cenci*

In searching out the background of Shelley's play *The Cenci*,[1] scholars have corroborated his assertion that he based it on an Italian manuscript[2] setting forth the late sixteenth-century murder of Count Francesco Cenci by members of his family and their subsequent execution. By good fortune we have access to Shelley's declared source, one of the versions of the Cenci legend,

---

[1] I am indebted to Professors Claude Flory and Harold C. Gross for bringing the existence of the Pieracci play to my attention in the latter's "Francesco da Rimini on Stage: An Annotated Bibliography of Primary and Secondary Sources," Diss. Florida State University, 1974, pp. 53–54. I also wish to acknowledge the cooperation of Associate Professor Richard Hilary and Professor Azzurra Givena of the Modern Language Department, Florida State University, in checking my translation of the Pieracci play. Both also supplied me with useful hints in tracking down Italian background.

[2] Shelley, Preface, *The Cenci*, in *The Complete Poetical Works of Percy Bysshe Shelley*, ed. Thomas Hutchinson (London: Oxford University Press, 1961), pp., 275–76. For seven accounts of the Cenci legend I am following the classification of Truman Guy Steffan, "Seven Accounts of the Cenci and Shelley's Drama," *Studies in English Literature 1500–1900*, 9 (1969), 601–18: A, B, C, D, Es, Es-1, F. Es, the account that Shelley drew upon, was published in English translation by Mary Shelley in 1840. I am using it as given in *The Works of Percy Bysshe Shelley*, ed. Harry Buxton Forman, 8 vols. (London: Reeves and Turner, 1880), II, 399–417.

a legend which was all that was available to Shelley since the Vatican did not release the true facts of the case until the middle of the nineteenth century.[3] Numerous echoes in Shakespeare and other Elizabethan and Jacobean playwrights, Calderon, and some contemporary English and Italian plays, as well as the shaping effect of Italian opera and the star system on the English stage, have also been detailed in scholarship that has enriched our apprehension of Shelley's mind at work.

No one has thus far noticed that in 1816, about three years before Shelley wrote his play, an Italian playwright named Vincenzio Pieracci published in Florence a volume of *Tragedie* containing four tragedies, among them a *Beatrice Cenci*.[4] Most

---

[3]For a more accurate historical account, consult Corrado Ricci, *Beatrice Cenci*, trans. Morris Bishop and Henry Longan Stuart, 2 vols. (New York: Boni and Liveright, 1925). Of the seven legendary accounts listed and treated by Steffan (see footnote 2 above), each account differs in many aspects from the others. When Mary, Shelley's widow, published an English translation of the account Shelley used, Es, in 1840, she omitted from it Count Cenci's supposed licentious attempts on his daughter Beatrice and the testimony of the laundress (Steffan, p. 603) about the blood on the bedsheets. When Shelley sent an English translation to Thomas Love Peacock in July, 1819 (see footnote 15 below), he did not mention the translator, nor did Mary later in her 1840 publication. The translator remains unknown. As Steffan says (p. 603), Es is not included in D. L. Clark's edition of Shelley's prose (*Shelley's Prose; or the Trumpet of a Prophecy* [Albuquerque: University of New Mexico Press, 1954]), and, adds Steffan, "The phrasing is frequently so awkward that one doubts that Mary or Percy was the translator." In his painstaking study of the seven legendary accounts at his disposal, Steffan (p. 607, n. 13) finds that Shelley did not draw upon any of them other than Es.

[4]*Beatrice Cenci* in *Tragedie di Vincenzio Pieracci di Turicchi* (Firenze: Presso Niccolo Carli, 1816), pp. 67–134. The following item appeared in the *Gazzetta di Firenze* #110, September 12, 1816, p. 4 [my translation]:

"There has come to light a volume of tragedies of Signor Vincenzio Pieracci of Turicchi, and they are *Michele di Lando, Beatrice Cenci, Francesca da Rimini* newly reproduced and entirely changed from the first draft by the author, and *Il Turno*. The restricted size of our page would not permit making known the merit, the serious delicacy of the plots chosen, and the happy denouement of this writer. However, desirous that the public may remain best informed of this, we will give hurriedly a sample idea of it, commencing with the first tragedy.

"Florence, because of its popular and patrician tempests, perpetrated as at Rome itself, saw all order, every law, put down, the security of the town in peril, and saw near the end of her existence actual and political, when, in the manner of Menenius Agrippa, she raised herself above the unsteady faction of the people, and saw Michele di Lando reuniting the two orders of the state, bearing lightning in these verses,

writers on Italian literature and drama make no mention of Pieracci,[5] though he had published an earlier volume of tragedies in
1798, brought out a volume of comedies in 1820, and published

---

Gentle I will be with honorable citizens,
But a horrendous fury armed with daggers
Against criminal souls who stand intent to
Disturb the peace of the oppressed country.

"In this tragedy, in the footsteps of Shakespeare, he has introduced the
personages of the common people, and he makes them speak from much
acquaintance with the usages and ancient customs of our Florence.

"The *Beatrice Cenci's* having been till now neglected by all the writers
made known that it did not provide a subject for the stage. Our author,
nevertheless, with much dexterity has rendered it in the mannher of the *Mirra*
of Alfieri not only tolerable in the theatre, but interesting, although Beatrice
may be stained with a crime more infamous.

"The *Francesca da Rimini* depicts marvelously the terrible struggles of an
enamored soul with great prestige and integrity to find excuse and compassion
on the part of her sorrowing parents until the vivid expressions of her love,
which has become a sentiment of crime.

"*Il Turno* finally presents the grandiose picture of a king who wishes to
die free, and to defend his country from foreign assaults in spite of all the
obstacles that beset him.

"Our author has sought in style to support the varying subjects and to
imitate nature, by making easy penetration into the secret streets of the human
heart. In sum, to a literate public he wishes to grant absolute judgment upon
the mentioned tragedies, which we cannot presume to do contrary to that idea
that we may have so hurriedly indicated.

"The above-mentioned tragedies are for sale at the printery Niccolò Carli
in Borgo SS Apostoli, and at the distribution center of the *Gazzetta* at the price
of four paoli."

[5]Since the account of Carlo del Balzo is the only one of the life and career of
Pieracci that has come to light, with the exception of some prefatory remarks
Pieracci has made about himself, included elsewhere, it appears below almost in
toto in my translation, with the omission of an irrelevant passage and with del
Balzo's footnotes in brackets, adjacent to the passages where they occur. Certain
discrepancies in the Italian should be pointed out: the playwright's given name
appears variously as Vincenzo and Vincenzio (the latter in a footnote to a passage I
have omitted); the four tragedies listed as written between 1811 and 1824 all
appeared in 1816; one early tragedy, *Valentiniano*, does not appear in the lists,
and *Garrick* is misspelled as *Garrik*.

Carlo del Balzo, ed., *Poesie di Mille Autori Intorno a Dante Alighieri* (Rome:
Forzani, 1903), VIII, 126-28:

"Vincenzo Pieracci was born March 14, 1768, of Antonio Pieracci and Gio-
vanna Pratesi in the county of Turicchi eighteen miles from Florence in the
valley of Sieve. His family descends from the old and noble Ranucci, whose
political misadventures constrained them to change their name during the

3

two final volumes of comedies in 1822.[6] Guido Mazzone, an exception, reaches back to Pieracci from his treatment of a much later period and resurrects his tragedies of 1816 as a literary

turbulent epoch of the factions. Banished from Florence, they lost status in the rural area and assumed the cognomen of Pieracci, which was in substance the ill-sounding genitive of a Piero who by works consistent with the nature of those times of troubles and parties was named Pieraccio.

"He learned Latin from a cousin, a famous Latinist, priest, and governor of the seminary of Fiesole.

"When he was very young, he entered the noble guards. Loving poetry and the classics, he began to write in verses that pleased the court of the Grand Dukes (1790).

"He went to Paris in 1811 with General Mattei. There he remained for various periods, visited then all of France, and, returning to Italy through the Simplon, he tarried also in Switzerland.

"He died February 22, 1834, and was buried in the cloister of Santa Croce under the large loggia that flanks the church.

"He was very much a lover of the fine arts, and from his youth studied with passion architecture and design. Of vast and profound erudition, he was facile also in learning the most difficult things. He was a man of virtue and integrity, of courage, of mind, and of heart firm in purposes, as well as generous.

"He wrote various short burlesque narrative poems in ottava rima, sonnets, epigrams, charades, madrigals, and the like.[1] [[1]"The first tragedy written by Pieracci was the *Francesca da Rimini*, then *Sorismonda, La Madre Maccabea, L'Almeone*, all in 1791; *Agrippina Maggiore* (1799). —*L'Etruria Liberata* (1799), a short narrative poem cited by Moreni. —Other tragedies written from 1811 to 1824: *Michele di Lando, Beatrice Cenci, Francesca da Rimini* (redone), *Turno*. —Comedies: *Dante Alighieri, Francesco Petrarca, Michelangiolo Buonarroti, Galileo Galilei, Ariosto, Tasso, Newton, Voltaire*. —Farces: *Il Magliabechi, Garrik*."]

* * * * *

"Before coming through the presses, the drama of Pieracci published by us [*Dante Alighieri*] has been performed with success in a good many cities of Tuscany.

"Pieracci was a member of various Academies of those times."[1] [[1]"These reports have been given by Major Vincenzo Pieracci, nephew of the poet, to my friend Count Paolo Galletti. I thank both."]

[6]The 1798 volume, Pieracci's first, has no publisher listed. The title page reads "Tragedie di Vincenzio Pieracci di Turicchi. Firenze MDCCXCVIII. Con Approvazione." The tragedies contained are *La Sorismonda, Valentiniano, La Madre Maccabea*, and *L'Almeone*. The third volume has on its title page *Commedie di Vincenzio Pieracci di Turicchi*. Firenze: Presso Niccolò Carli, 1820. The plays it contains are *Dante Alighieri, Francesco Petrarca, Michelangiolo Buonarroti*, and *Galileo Galilei*. The fourth collection, in two volumes, is *Commedie di*

"curiosità."[7] Pieracci had conceived of the four—*Michele di Lando, Beatrice Cenci, Francesca da Rimini,* and *Turno*—as exemplars of the four degrees of which the buskin is capable. The *Beatrice Cenci* was to exemplify the domestic tragedy.[8] Shelley was no stranger to Italian.

The years Shelley spent in Italy "increased his sensitiveness and enthusiasm for Italian poetry," says Neville Rogers, and his Italian studies "went, in fact, far deeper than his studies in Spanish and German." He attempted composition in Italian—for example, poems addressed to Emilia Viviani—and he made translations into English. His translations "directly or indirectly . . . usually connect somehow with his composition."[9]

Pieracci has dropped so far out of sight on the road from the past that a modern Italian critic calls Shelley's the first dramatic version of the Cenci story,[10] but in 1819 the *Beatrice Cenci* was

---

Vincenzio Piueracci di Turicchi. Firenze: Presso Niccolò Carli, M.DCCC.XXII. Volume I had *Lodovico Ariosto, Torquato Tasso,* and *Il Magliabechi.* Volume II has *Isacco Neuton, Francesco di Voltaire,* and *Garrick.*

[7]*Ottocento* (Milano: Casa Editrice Dr. Francesco Vallardi, 1934), II, 953.

[8]Aristotle said that tragic characters must be persons of importance to the state. Using this as his basis in the "Scope of the Author" (no page numbers), prefatory to the 1816 volume, Pieracci states and exemplifies his doctrine for the classification of tragedies. Beginning with the first play, *Michele di Lando,* he gradually raises the stature of the main characters through four degrees. The fact that Michele was a wool worker moves his play close to comedy, but his nobility of character saves him for tragedy. *Beatrice Cenci* establishes the measure of the second degree, in which the characters are to be esteemed as bordering on the character of the non-public, private gentleman. *Francesca da Rimini,* of the third degree, has characters of known merit, better suiting the decorum of Greek doctrine. *Il Turno,* of the fourth degree, has characters of the highest stature, best suiting the "specific conditions" of the high issue of tragedy.

[9]Neville Rogers, *Shelley at Work: A Critical Inquiry* (Oxford: Clarendon Press, 1956), pp. 232–33, 241–47.

[10]Giovanni Marchi, "La Tragedia dei Cenci nelle Opere Teatrali," *Nuova Antologia,* 503 (August 1968), 545. That a playwright who published eighteen plays over a period of twenty-four years should be so little remembered as to be omitted from the many huge volumes of the biographically oriented *Enciclopedia Italiana* is bound to excite curiosity and conjecture. Pieracci's own words are at least prophetic. In the Preface to the 1798 volume (pp. III–IX) he notes that great creators seldom give rise to successors as great. Without making the connection, he says he has followed in the footsteps of the great tragic playwright Vittorio Alfieri because Alfieri has shown the necessity of such a style as his. Of his own beginnings, Pieracci says, "I must . . . confess that I became without wishing it the

author of two tragedies. They found a public so indulgent in their favor that it wished to put them in circulation exempt from that criticism accustomed to draw with it some production provided that it is a daughter of the human spirit." Once having begun, there was nothing for it but to continue. He had evidently obtained for his early plays a *succès d'estime*, but plays ask something more, as Pieracci indicates. He ventures "to predict for them the destiny of first performances." One play, the *Dante Alighieri* (1820), was, according to the biographical account (note 5), "performed with success in a good many cities of Tuscany." For the other plays I can find no evidence of production.

Twenty-four years after the first volume, in the Preface (pp. 3–8) of his final collection, addressed to his young son Pietro Iperide, he addresses in retrospect some of the same themes as in his 1798 Preface, but now with a rueful tone suggestive of failure. He warns his son against a literary career, regrets his own confinement to the shadow of Alfieri, and wishes he had instead attempted comedy. If your father, he says, "had sooner put on the sock, who knows that the half-extinguished ashes of the Adriatic Terence would not have revived on the banks of the Arno!"

A discussion of Pieracci's *Dante Alighieri* by C. Levi, "Dante 'Dramatis Persona,'" *Archivio Storico Italiano*, Anno LXXXIX (Firenze: R. Deputazione di Storia Patria, 1921), I, 126–29, may provide a clue as to why Italians have not cherished the works and memory of Pieracci. After giving him credit as "the first Italian dramatic poet who may have written a work dedicating it to Dante," Levi proceeds to demolish the play. He says it is full of bad verses, anachronisms, vulgarisms, and historical inaccuracies. Pieracci has Dante present for his trial in Florence, imprisoned, and finally sentenced to banishment. An Italian colleague of mine says of such a bold departure from the familiar biography of a revered figure, "He touched the untouchable." Pieracci specialized in plays about celebrated personages of history, and it is safe to say that no account, legendary or historical, known or unknown, could sanction a Beatrice Cenci who, having no clear connection with her father's murder, commits suicide to take the blame for it. Yet this is Pieracci's treatment. Where does artistic reconstruction of history cease and falsification begin? Pieracci seems also to have been the first to give dramatic treatment to the Cenci story. The reviewer of the *Gazzetta di Firenze* (note 4) attributes the long neglect to the infamous crime of Beatrice, which had rendered the subject unfit for the stage. He gives Pieracci credit for his "dexterity," which has rendered the subject "tolerable in the theatre" in the manner of Alfieri's *Mirra*, whose heroine commits suicide after having fallen in love sensually with her own father. Shelley had read the life of Alfieri, in Italian, in 1814, and Alfieri's tragedies in 1815; Newman Ivey White, *Shelley* (New York: Alfred A. Knopf, 1940) II, 540–41. Mary Shelley in 1818 had entertained plans of translating the above play of Alfieri (White, II, 37).

Another contemporary reviewer of the four tragedies of 1816, in "Tragedie di Vincenzo Pieracci di Turicchi, Firenze, Carli 1816," *Giornale di Letteratura e Belle Arti* (Firenze, 1816), I, 127–32, is little more favorable than Levi was later to be. He says that the *Turno* alone has a subject worthy of contact with those of the tragic writers. He satirizes Pieracci's four gradations of tragedy as fit for the unlearned who esteem a corpse in state according to the number of candles about it (p. 128). After some pages of quotations from the plays, he says the author is one "who perhaps having wished to imitate Shakespeare is more trivial than he, but has not the least elevation that approaches the sublimity of that tragedian" (p. 132).

still new from the press and had been published in a city and area of Italy that Shelley frequented at that time. Although Shelley himself makes no mention of an Italian play on the subject,[11] the numerous instances of unacknowledged sources in Shelley—and one might add in Shakespeare, Byron, Picasso, and multitudinous others—makes this omission no surprise. The construction so often put upon one's having sources, a fact of which Shelley was well aware,[12] makes for few creative artists as frank about them as Kipling in "When 'Omar Smote 'is Bloomin' Lyre." A reading of both plays puts it beyond reasonable doubt, I think, that Shelley did draw upon Pieracci's *Beatrice Cenci.*

"On my arrival at Rome," Shelley says in the Preface to *The Cenci*, "I found that the story of the Cenci was a subject not to be mentioned in Italian society without awakening a deep and breathless interest." Undoubtedly someone at this time brought the Pieracci play to his attention.[13] The story itself was universally

---

[11]Lists of Shelley's reading in F. L. Jones, ed., *Mary Shelley's Journal* (Norman: University of Oklahoma Press, 1947), pp. 218–31; and Newman Ivey White, *Shelley*, II, 539–45, do not show Pieracci's play. I have not found mention of Pieracci in my own check of likely sources for such a name, including, among others, Roger Ingpen and W. E. Peck, eds., *The Complete Works of Percy Bysshe Shelley*, 10 vols. (New York: Scribner's, 1926–30); W. E. Peck, *Shelley: His Life and Work*, 2 vols. (Boston: Houghton Mifflin, 1927); F. L. Jones, ed., *Shelley's Letters*, 2 vols. (Oxford: Clarendon Press, 1964); Thomas Medwin, *The Life of Percy Bysshe Shelley* (London: Oxford University Press, 1913); Thomas Jefferson Hogg, *The Life of Shelley* in *The Life of Percy Bysshe Shelley* (New York: E. P. Dutton & Co., 1933); Thomas Love Peacock, *Memoirs of Shelley* in *The Life of Percy Bysshe Shelley* (New York: E. P. Dutton & Co., 1933); Kenneth Neill Cameron and D. H. Reiman, eds., *Shelley and His Circle*, 6 vols. (Cambridge: Harvard University Press, 1961–   ); and Marion Kingston Stocking, ed., *The Journals of Claire Clairmont* (Cambridge: Harvard University Press, 1968).

[12]In a footnote to the Preface to *The Cenci*, Shelley says he was indebted for "a most sublime passage in *El Purgatorio de San Patricio* of Calderon; the only plagiarism which I have intentionally committed in the whole piece" (p. 277). Shelley may have thought Pieracci's innovations historically based.

[13]Preface, p. 276. It would be well to trace Shelley's connection with the Cenci story in time and place in order best to decide when and where he probably first knew of Pieracci's play. Shelley says at the beginning of his Preface to *The Cenci* (p. 275), "A Manuscript was communicated to me during my travels in Italy, which was copied from the archives of the Cenci Palace at Rome, and contains a detailed account of the horrors which ended in the extinction of one of the noblest and richest families of that city during the Pontificate of Clement VIII, in the year 1599." Between March 30, 1818, when they first entered Italy, and May 25,

known: "All ranks of people knew the outlines of this history, and participated in the overwhelming interest which it seems to have the magic of exciting in the human heart."[14]

The possibility that some other playwright might anticipate

1818, when we may date the first connection with the Cenci story, the Shelleys traveled about a great deal, visiting Turin, Milan, Pisa, and Leghorn. It was apparently during these travels that Shelley received the Cenci manuscript he speaks of, and on May 25, while they were at Leghorn, Mary finished copying the manuscript history of Beatrice Cenci that later supplied the basis for *The Cenci*; White, *Shelley*, II, 6–18. From May, 1818, till Shelley began writing *The Cenci*, about a year elapsed. During this long period of gestation, the Shelleys moved about a great deal. They spent nine weeks of the summer at Bagni di Lucca in the Apennines, socializing little, reading much, and horseback riding. On August 20, Shelley, traveling with Claire Clairmont, passed through Florence on their way to Venice. The stay was too brief to give ground for conjecture of contact with Pieracci or his play. In September and October Shelley moved between Este and Venice preoccupied with personal problems and sorrows. In the latter part of November the Shelleys stopped for a week of sightseeing in Rome. At the end of November they began a three-month stay in Naples. On March 5, 1819 began their momentous stay in Rome (White, II, 18–84).

It was almost certainly here and now, at Rome, and not earlier, that Shelley experienced the stimuli that led to the composition of the long-gestating *Cenci*. On April 14, at a visit to the Colonna Palace, Shelley saw the supposed portrait of Beatrice Cenci by Guido that moved him to the emotional utterance recorded in the Preface (p. 278). On May 11 the Shelley party visited the Cenci palace. Meanwhile, during April, Shelley and Mary and Claire visited two or three times a week the famous salon of the elderly bluestocking Signora Mariana Candida Dionigi frequented by Italian and foreign literati of wide-ranging interests. It was in this "Italian society" at Rome that Shelley's mention of the Cenci story must have drawn the "deep and breathless interest" recorded in the Preface (p. 276). Undoubtedly one or more of the people the Shelley party socialized with in the salon and out of it brought to Shelley's attention Pieracci's *Beatrice Cenci*, published a little less than three years before in Florence. Shelley began to write apparently on May 14. He continued the writing at Villa Valsovano, between Leghorn and Monte Nero, from June 17 until he finished about August 8, 1819; White, II, 88–91, 100; *Mary Shelley's Journal*, pp. 118–22; Marion Kingston Stocking, ed., *The Journals of Claire Clairmont*, pp. 102–11.

[14]Hutchinson, ed., p. 276. Clarence Stratton, "The Cenci Story in Literature and in Fact," in *Studies in English Drama*, ed. Allison Gaw, First Series (New York: Appleton, 1917), p. 159, suggests a more mundane reason for the survival of the Cenci story besides its beautiful girl on the scaffold: "There was a line of collateral relatives to which part of the great estate of the Cenci family should have reverted." It was all confiscated by the Church. "The . . . motive of resentment . . . endured. Hardly had Pope Clement died when the cry went up from these disappointed relatives, '*Li hanno spogliati.*' And from the beginning, with romantic additions that quite overshadowed the repulsive facts, grew the Cenci story of literature."

him with the public excited a great deal of nervousness in Shelley. In July, 1819, he addressed a letter to Thomas Love Peacock, urging him to investigate the possibility of a stage presentation. "Write to me as soon as you can on this subject because it is necessary that I should present it, or if rejected by the Theatre, print it this coming season lest some body else should get hold of it, as the story which now exists only in Mss begins to be generally known among the English. . . . Of course you will not show the Mss. [an English translation of the Italian MS] to any one—and write to me by return of Post at which time the play will be ready to be sent."[15] The existence of a recent Italian play no doubt sharpened his anxiety. In September he wrote his publisher, Charles Ollier, that he was sending the work already printed.[16]

Under the influence of the greatest of Italian tragic poets, Vittorio Alfieri (1749–1803), Italian tragedy at the end of the eighteenth century and well into the nineteenth was neoclassical in form, a heritage of the French seventeenth century.[17] It had absorbed into its content another French importation, this time of the eighteenth century, the lachrymose drama also known as the bourgeois, or family, tragedy. The *Beatrice Cenci* was Pieracci's contribution to this genre. Passions, sentimentality, and tears, in a neoclassical mold, dominate the Italian theatre of the time.[18] Confined as it is within the unities of time, place, and action, Alfierian tragedy offers as its hallmarks a reduction of personages, a conflict of individual forces, a battle against tyranny, much emphasis on morality, and clipped, abbreviated language.[19] The Cenci story was made to order for Alfierian treatment, and Pieracci's *Beatrice Cenci* is Alfierian to the last degree.

As the first act opens, Beatrice is deep in melancholy over

<hr>

[15]*Letters*, II, 103.

[16]*Letters*, II, 116–17.

[17]Joseph S. Kinnard, *The Italian Theatre: From the Close of the Seventeenth Century* (New York: William Edwin Rudge, 1932), pp. 125, 150–51. Bruno Maier, *Il Neoclassicismo* (Palermo: Palumbo, 1946), pp. 8–9, dates the neoclassical period from 1789 to 1815.

[18]Kinnard, pp. 128–29.

[19]Francesco de Sanctis, *History of Italian Literature*, trans. Joan Redfern (New York: Harcourt, Brace and Company, 1931), pp. 888, 890–98.

the death of her father, Francesco Cenci, and Cammillo Farnese, a man of sixty who has a fatherly affection for her, is trying in vain to persuade her to go abroad with him for the relief of her sorrow. Ippolito Guerra, who seems to be in love with her (an interest not pressed in the play), brings word that the Sovereign of Rome entertains the suspicion that Francesco did not hurl himself from the balcony to his death on the precipitous rock. He has had the body exhumed for examination. In the course of the dialogue Cammillo refers to the terrible deeds of Francesco, who has done evil to others. At the head of a band of soldiers, Fausto, on orders, comes to place Beatrice under house arrest. In Act II Marsilio, the judge, makes arrangements for a trial of Beatrice at the same place, the Palazzo Cenci. The people of Rome, believing her guilty, are reported clamoring to see her. During Act III Ippolito, who enters to Beatrice disguised as a servant, attempts in vain to persuade her to escape by a garden gate. Cammillo, admitted by his influence with the Sovereign, talks with Beatrice of her father's mistreatment of her and of an early petition for relief she had written to the Sovereign that has never been delivered until today. At the trial in Act IV, Olimpio and Marzio, the presumed mur-derers, are brought in, and Olimpio's testimony, with the help of Marzio's, implicates Beatrice in the incitement to murder and even in the stabbing of Francesco after his death. Beatrice denies know-ing them, though they had been servants to the Cenci, and, by implication, denies having given a mantle to Marzio as reward for the murder. Realizing that they themselves are to be found guilty, and shaken by her stand, Olimpio and Marzio, under the leader-ship of Marzio, retract their incrimination of Beatrice. Marsilio, the judge, has already contributed to the exoneration of Beatrice by pointing out a discrepancy in Olimpio's account: the body showed three, not four, stab wounds. Olimpio and Marzio alone are judged guilty. Beatrice refuses once more to go abroad with Cammillo. In Act V Olimpio and Marzio, now doomed, are allowed a final interview with Beatrice. Marzio asks her to take care of his aged mother, who has been living on scraps from the Cenci table. This plea is decisive with Beatrice. She calls the servants together, divides a great deal of property among them, and takes leave of them. After they have gone she drinks poison and sends for Marsilio. She tells him and her friends that she alone is guilty, and as the curtain falls she is still standing, but the end is near.

The legendary account of the Cenci in Es, Shelley's primary source, is in many respects similar to other accounts written at the time of the executions in best representing what any and all could witness publicly and least reliable in what, in the absence of open records, had to be taken from rumors.

Francesco Cenci, an immensely wealthy Roman nobleman, lived in wickedness and debauchery. "Sodomy was the least, and atheism the greated" (p. 399) of his vices. He three times escaped the death sentence for sodomy by paying the Pope, Clement VIII, 100,000 crowns each time. He sent two of his sons, Rocco and Cristofero, to the University of Salamanca, but refused to maintain them until at their plea the Pope forced him to do so. His sons tried to remove their father by asking the Pope to condemn him, but the Pope refused. Francesco beat his two daughters until at the petition of the elder of the two the Pope married her off, with a dowry forced from Francesco. He rejoiced when Cristofero and Rocco were murdered, and refused to contribute to their funeral expenses. He compelled his remaining daughter, Beatrice, to witness his sexual antics with women in his house. Since Beatrice was grown and beautiful, "he tried to persuade the poor girl, by an enormous heresy, that children born of the commerce of a father with his daughter were all saints, and that the saints who obtained the highest places in Paradise had been thus born" (pp. 401–02). He beat her for her resistance to his desires. Like her sister, she petitioned the Pope, without effect, and later it was "pretended that [the petition] never came before the Pope" (p. 402).

In time Beatrice and her stepmother, Lucretia, Francesco's second wife, began to plan his death. They were assisted in this by Monsignore Guerra, a young man who visited the Cenci women and was sympathetic with their plight. Beatrice's elder brother, Giacomo, whose family Francesco had refused adequate support, was drawn into the scheme. For the actual murder, two disaffected vassals of Francesco, Marzio and Olimpio, were engaged.

Since the family was to spend the summer at the rock castle of Petrella, banditti of the vicinity were hired to dispose of Francesco. The plan miscarried when Francesco passed by at an unexpected time. It was decided that Marzio and Olimpio, to be paid a thousand crowns in installments, would murder Francesco in the castle. On September 9, 1598, after Francesco had fallen into a deep sleep from opium mixed in his drink, the murderers entered his room but balked at killing a sleeping old man. Beatrice threatened to do the deed herself and also threatened their lives. This time they killed him with a nail driven into his brain via his eye and another into his neck. After wrapping the body in a sheet, the ladies dropped it from a gallery into a garden, to substantiate a story that he had fallen through a weak spot in the gallery. While the family was in Rome, the Court of Naples became suspicious and discovered some discrepancies in the story. The Court of Rome was informed. Monsignore Guerra decided to have Marzio and Olimpio murdered to keep them from confessing. He succeeded with Olimpio, but Marzio escaped, was imprisoned, and confessed everything. Lucretia, Beatrice, and Giacomo were arrested, as was Bernardo, a younger brother of Beatrice. Having heard that one of the assassins he had hired to kill Olimpio had been arrested and had confessed, Monsignore Guerra escaped from Rome disguised as a charcoal man. Giacomo, Bernardo, and Lucretia confessed under torture, but Beatrice, under threat of torture, would make only an ambiguous confession. All were condemned. While the Pope was considering the pleas for mercy, notably the extenuating circumstances brought out by the advocate Farinacci, Paolo Santa Croce murdered his mother and escaped. With this as an example, the Pope ordered the executions. On Saturday, May 11, 1599, while the scaffold was being prepared on the bridge of S. Angelo, Bernardo was pardoned as innocent but sentenced to witness the executions of the other three. Then followed the gathering of the procession, Beatrice's writing of her will, descriptions of the garments of the ladies, some accidents among the crowd, the last words on the scaffold, the gory details of the beheadings, and the funerals. The account ends with descriptions of each of the four Cenci and the later life of Bernardo.

Since Shelley's *Cenci* is well known, a rapid summary of its plot should suffice to make intelligible what will be brought out later. During a career of wickedness and debauchery, Count

Francesco Cenci, head of one of the leading families of Rome, has compounded his crimes at great expense with the Pope, who is ruler of Rome. He hates his children, largely because of their expense, and celebrates the death of two of his sons, Rocco and Cristofano [sic]. His daughter Beatrice has attempted in vain to escape him. Just before the beginning of the third act he rapes Beatrice—a fact which is brought out gradually from her distraction. A plot is devised to murder Cenci that involves Beatrice, her stepmother Lucretia, her brother Giacomo, and a priest Orsino, who, with designs on Beatrice, becomes prime mover. When a first attempt by hired banditti on the road to Petrella fails, Olimpio and Marzio, two servants who hate Cenci, are engaged. After at first balking at killing a sleeping old man, under Beatrice's incitement they finally strangle him and drop his body over a balcony. Olimpio dies fighting papal officers who have come on another matter, and Marzio confesses, implicating the Cenci. Orsino escapes, and a younger brother of Beatrice, Bernardo, is not implicated. Lucretia and Giacomo confess, and under their pleading Beatrice makes an ambiguous confession. As the curtain falls all three are on their way to the scaffold.

When Shelley explains why he departs from his sources in *Prometheus Unbound*, he defends the creative process that must have governed his writing of *The Cenci* as well:

> The Greek tragic writers, in selecting as their subject any portion of their national history or mythology, employed in their treatment of it a certain arbitrary discretion. They by no means conceived themselves bound to adhere to the common interpretation or to imitate in story as in title their rivals and predecessors. Such a system would have amounted to a resignation of those claims to preference over their competitors which incited the composition. . . . I have presumed to employ a similar licence (pp. 204–05).

How did he use his sources? Neville Rogers, who has made a study of Shelley's mind at work in his use of sources, says that Shelley did not bring in such materials by a process of "patchwork . . . but rather one of absorption, transmutation, and, in the end, creation—creation of the most original kind."[20] In writing *The*

---

[20]Rogers, p. 154.

Cenci, he brought the same freedom of creativity to his sources as Shakespeare did to the *Ur-Hamlet*. His use of source is not all or nothing. The portions of Pieracci not used by Shelley are as much a part of the slag heap of his creativity as are the unused portions of his Italian manuscript, later published in English translation and now designated as Es. What matters is that Shelley evidently used considerable substance from Pieracci's *Beatrice Cenci* and that his use allows insight into his creative process. Es, which he follows in general for the development of his play, remains his primary source, and Pieracci becomes a secondary source. Truman Guy Steffan finds no evidence that he drew upon any of the other six versions of the Cenci legend that he has examined. On the whole Shelley departs from his Italian source for the Cenci legend far less than Pieracci must have done from his version or versions of the legend.[21]

It must be sufficiently obvious that what the creative artist does not use in a source in no wise affects the validity as a source of what he does use. If beyond reasonable doubt a poet uses one passage from a work by another, the other work becomes to that extent a source. The unused remainder is irrelevant, regardless of its extent, except insofar as it reveals the poet's creative selectivity in not using it. Although Shelley says in a footnote to the Preface that the only "intentionally committed" plagiarism in *The Cenci* is the use of a passage from Calderon, any reader acquainted with Shakespeare will recognize many echoes from the Bard, and there is a large bibliography of articles on Shelley's use of Shakespeare in *The Cenci* as well as elsewhere.[22] As with Shelley's use of Pieracci, we need not account for the great remainder of Shake-

---

[21]See notes 2, 3, and 10.

[22]The list of writings on Shelley's debt to Shakespeare, mainly in *The Cenci*, is long: *Shakespeare Society Papers*, 1, Article 13 (London, 1844), 52–54; "Some Notes on Othello," *Cornhill Magazine*, 18 (October 1868), 419–40; [J. S. Baynes], "Rossetti's Edition of Shelley," *Edinburgh Review*, 133, No. 262 (April 1871), 440–48; Leslie H. Allen, *Die Persönlichkeit P. B. Shelleys* (Leipzig: Bereiter, 1907); Ernest Sutherland Bates, *A Study of Shelley's Drama The Cenci* (New York: Columbia University Press, 1908), pp. 54–56; *The Cenci*, ed. George Woodberry, Belles Lettres Series (Boston: D. C. Heath, 1909), p. xxx; Carl Grabo, *The Magic Plant* (Chapel Hill: University of North Carolina Press, 1936), p. 304; Newman Ivey White, *The Unextinguished Hearth* (Durham: Duke University Press, 1938), p. 206, 209; David Lee Clark, "Shelley and Shakespeare," *PMLA*, 54 (1939),

261–87; Newman Ivey White, *Shelley* (New York: Knopf, 1940), I, 278; II, 217, 296, 420, 599; Sara Ruth Watson, "Shelley and Shakespeare: An Addendum: A Comparison of *Othello* and *The Cenci*," *PMLA*, 55 (1940), 611–14; Frederick L. Jones, "Shelley and Shakespeare: A Supplement," *PMLA*, 59 (1944), 591–96; Carlos Baker, *Shelley's Major Poetry: The Fabric of a Vision* (Princeton: Princeton University Press, 1948), 209n.; Beach Langston, "Shelley's Use of Shakespeare," *Huntington Library Quarterly*, 12, No. 2 (1949), 163–90; E. M. M. Taylor, "Shelley and Shakespeare," *Essays in Criticism*, 3, No. 3 (1953), 367–68; Robert Fricker, "Shakespeare and das Englische Romantische Drama," *Shakespeare Jahrbuch*, eds. Herman Heuer, Wolfgang Clemen, Rudolf Stamm, 95 (Heidelberg: Quelle & Meyer, 1959), 72–76; Earl R. Wasserman, "Shakespeare and the English Romantic Movement," *The Persistence of Shakespeare Idolatry* (Detroit: Wayne State University, 1964), pp. 77–103; Stuart Curran, *Shelley's Cenci: Scorpions Ringed with Fire* (Princeton: Princeton University Press, 1970), pp. 35–36, n. 2.

Langston, p. 170, says "Shelley relied upon Shakespeare consciously or unconsciously—and almost surely both. . . ." He "relied upon the reading he so purposely did in the poetry and drama of Shakespeare [in the months before writing] to give poetic and dramatic form to the subject matter he found in the manuscript. . . ." On the areas of indebtedness, Langston says (p. 188), "Shelley borrowed his Shakespearean materials in all quantities—phrases, brief images, larger and more fully developed images; whole scenes (such as the principal borrowings in *The Cenci* from *Macbeth* and *Othello*), and even whole structural outlines (such as the structural principle of *The Cenci*. . . .)."

Following are some of the many parallel phrases and images noted by critics between various plays of Shakespeare and *The Cenci*.

Shakespeare	*The Cenci*
Othello	
V, ii, 7–13 — "Put out the light."	III, ii, 11–18, 51–53 — "Thou small flame. . . ." "And yet once quenched I cannot thus relume/ My Father's life."

(*Cornhill*, pp. 430–31; Bates, pp. 54–55; Watson, pp. 611–12; Langston, p. 169)

I, iii, 230–32 — "thrice-driven bed of down."	II, ii, 12–16 — "thrice-driven beds of down.

(Langston, p. 168)

V, ii, 303–04 — "From this time forth I never will speak word."	V, iii, 89 — "No other pains shall force another word."

(Bates, p. 55)

King Lear	
I, v, 50–51 — "Oh, let me not be mad, not mad, sweet Heaven!"	V, iv, 56–57 — "Let me not go mad!/ Sweet Heaven . . ."

(*Cornhill*, p. 432; Bates, p. 55; Clark, p. 279)

II, iv, 285 — "they shall be the terrors of the earth."	IV, i, 92 — "Her name shall be the terror of the earth."

(Clark, p. 278)

I, iv, 303–11—Lear's curse on Goneril that she should have a "child of spleen."

IV, i, 141–46—Cenci's curse on Beatrice that her offspring should be "a hideous likeness of herself."

(Bates, p. 54; Clark, pp. 282–84; Langston, p. 169; Fricker, p. 72)

Macbeth

III, iv, 21–23—"I had else been perfect,/ Whole as the marble, founded as the rock,/ As broad and general as the casing air."

IV, iv, 46–51—"The deed is done. . . . I am . . ./ Free as the earth-surrounding air . . . Consequence, to me,/ Is as the wind which strikes the solid rock. . . ."

([Baynes], p. 447)

II, ii, 35—"Methought I heard a voice cry, 'Sleep no more'!"

V, iii, 6—"Methinks that I shall never sleep again."

(Clark, p. 279)

I, v, 46–48—"no compunctious visitings of nature . . . keep peace between the effect and it."

II, ii, 130–31—"Could . . . despise . . . all/ That frowns between my wish and its effect."

(Langston, p. 168)

Hamlet

III, i, 67—"When we have shuffled off this mortal coil."

II, i, 86–87—"all this hideous coil/ Shall be remembered. . . ."

(Langston, p. 168)

I, iii, 78–80—"To thine own self be true."

IV, iv, 40—"Be faithful to thyself."

(Bates, p. 55)

Measure for Measure

III, i, 119—"To lie in cold obstruction and to rot."

V, iv, 49–50—"So young to go/ Under the obscure, cold, rotting, wormy ground!"

(Bates, p. 55)

Richard II

I, iii, 194–96—"By this time, had the king permitted us,/ One of our souls had wandered in the air,/ Banished this frail sepulchre of our flesh."

III, i, 26–28—"These putrefying limbs/ Shut round and sepulchre the panting soul/ Which would burst forth into the wandering air!"

(Langston, p. 168)

Richard III

IV, i, 83–84—"Never . . . Have I enjoyed the golden dew of sleep."

Julius Caesar

II, i, 230—"Enjoy the honey-heavy dew of slumber."

}

V, iii, 7–8—"I must shake the heavenly dew of rest/ From . . . ."

(Langston, p. 169)

speare not represented in *The Cenci*, or regard it as invalidating the echoes that do appear.

Shelley omits a great deal of his acknowledged source in the legend, but it remains nonetheless his primary source. Shelley has been quoted on his independent use of sources in the Preface to *Prometheus Unbound*, and Neville Rogers in his judgment that Shelley's procedure with sources was one of "adsorption, transmutation, and, in the end, creation—creation of a most original kind." In fact, we cannot always be certain that Shelley's divergences from Pieracci do not represent his independent reactions against and reshaping of Pieraccian materials, his carrying them beyond the point of immediate recognition.

Though there is a great deal of his acknowledged Italian source, Es, that Shelley does not use and a great deal of Pieracci as well, our main interest will be in what Shelley could find in Pieracci and not in Es, as well as what this signifies of his creative interests and methods. First let us look at what he did not use of Pieracci and what the departures signify. A large proportion of the differences are those to be expected between a neoclassical, and Alfierian, drama on the one hand and a romantic drama, such as Shakespeare's, on the other. Both playwrights in their own ways compress the historical time span of the Cenci murder. Es, which Shelley follows, itself compresses the historical events of about three years (1596–1599) into about one year. Since he is writing in the neoclassical manner—fitting his play to the unities of time, place, and action—Pieracci compresses much more than

---

For larger parallels, perhaps the most telling are between *Macbeth* and *The Cenci*. The lines in the murder scenes of the two plays (*Macbeth*, II, ii, 10–20; *The Cenci*, IV, iii, 5–44) are closely parallel, with their strange sounds, failures of will, and similar, staccato phrasing (Bates, p. 54; Clark, pp. 284–85; Langston, p. 169). After the murder there is an immediate arrival of untimely guests in both plays (*Macbeth*, II, ii, 59–74; *The Cenci*, IV, iii, 57–65) (Clark, pp. 285–86). Both Lady Macbeth and Lucretia faint, or seem to, after the murder and among the new arrivals (*Macbeth*, II, iii, 132; *The Cenci*, IV, iv, 175) (Clark, p. 286). The interrupted banquet scene staged by Macbeth (III, iv, 32–120) suggests the one staged by Francesco Cenci (I, iii, 1–164) (Bates, p. 54; Langston, p. 169; Fricker, p. 72).

This note is lengthy, but could be much longer, with many more citations of parallels. Whatever the reason for Shelley's reticence, Shakespeare and Pieracci are entitled to recognition, with the acknowledged Es, as part of the background of *The Cenci*.

Shelley.[23] The action of Pieracci's play accords with the neo-classical unity of time by taking place in one day or less and after the murder of Francesco Cenci. Since the death, or approaching death, of Beatrice is essential to the drama, Cenci's death would have to be in the past, to be covered in a relatively undramatic fashion by narrations of the characters. Francesco Cenci is dead and buried as the play opens. There is no indication that the exhumation and autopsy, which begin within the first few pages, take any particular time. Events move fast chronologically (though the dramatic pace is slow). In Act III, Scene iv (p. 71) Camillo tells Beatrice that the Sovereign has received and read her petition to him, written eight months earlier, only this day. At the end of the second act Beatrice's trial is to begin within an hour. The trial and verdict occur in the fourth act; and the only indication of time lapse as the fifth act opens is that the delayed sentence of death for Marzio and Olimpio has been rendered. Immediately after the scenes with the doomed men and the servants, Beatrice drinks poison with the remark to herself that she will not be living in an hour. She is still alive when the curtain falls.

With more time at his disposal, and, so, with less reason to depart from the legend, Shelley could spend the first three acts developing the dramatic conflict between Cenci and his daughter Beatrice as well as the other members of the family. He could devote the last two acts to the murder and the dramatic conflict between Beatrice and the papal court.

In the rough draft of his Preface Shelley says, "The story is much the same in the tragedy as in the manuscript except that in the latter [sic] the action is hurried more hurried & that Orsino—whose real name was Guerra—plays a more conspicuous part."[24] Whether or not Shelley is compromising between Es and Pieracci, there is an estimate by Professor Paul Smith that Shelley compresses the action of *The Cenci* to two or three weeks: Acts I and II cover two consecutive days in the middle of January 1599; III and

---

[23]Steffan, pp. 607–08, n. 13, notes Shelley's compression of the time span.
[24]*Note Books of Percy Bysshe Shelley*, ed. H. Buxton Forman (Boston: The Bibliophile Society, 1911), II, 94, n. 86.

IV, three consecutive days about a week later; and V, about a week soon after.[25]

To satisfy the unity of place, which is dependent upon the unity of time, Pieracci has all of the action in the house of Beatrice; whereas Shelley, with less reason to depart from the legend, moves the action about to various places in Rome and lays the fourth act in Petrella, a castle in the Apulian Apennines. Most of these changes of scene are necessary if, unlike Pieracci, he is to follow the legendary narrative in chronological order. The confrontations occur in Rome; the murder occurs in Petrella; and the trial, imprisonment, and executions take place in Rome.

Neoclassical concentration on central theme probably induced Pieracci to limit the narrated murder to one successful attempt; however, Shelley, evidently desirous of building as many secondary scenes of tension as dramatically possible, includes the unsuccessful attempt by the bandits on the road to Petrella. To the same intent are his surprise entrances: approaching footsteps turn out to be not those of the expected Cenci but of a servant, or of Giacomo. Immediately after the murder a horn announces not the expected "tedious guest" but the accusatory papal Legate.

Nothing better illustrates the similar, yet diversified, compression of time in the two plays than the treatment of the varying off-stage time lapses between the murderer's, or murderers', confession, which implicates Beatrice, and Beatrice's "confession." In Es there is considerable time between Marzio's confession in Naples and his retraction and death in Rome "overcome and moved by the presence of mind and courage of Beatrice." Her "lively eloquence" that "confused the judges" and her confession come still later by some months.[26] In Pieracci, once Olimpio and Marzio begin their confession, which they make in the presence of Beatrice, the action is continuous until they retract their implication of her and Beatrice is exonerated. Here Pieracci introduces a

[25]"Restless Casuistry: Shelley's Composition of *The Cenci*," *KSJ*, 13 (1964), 82; 82, n. 19.

[26]Curran, pp. 44–46, notes Shelley's adherence here to Es and his elimination of time gaps.

very short time lapse, to which is added some minor action: then Beatrice takes poison and assumes the burden of guilt. In Shelley Beatrice is not present for Marzio's confession, but she is brought in a few moments later, and in continuous action she presses him till he retracts, and he dies. At this point as in Pieracci, Shelley provides a short pause and Beatrice makes her final confession in a separate action. Underlying the similarities and differences of detail the chief parallel of Pieracci to Shelley in off-stage compression of time is structural. Pieracci compresses the time of his play to something like the time of the action on stage, evidently conforming to the neoclassical conception that this best serves verisimilitude. With Pieracci probably before him, and the many examples of compression in Shakespeare, Shelley telescopes the time, makes the action "more hurried," to increase the tempo and to heighten the sense that the action and the outcome are linked in inevitability.

Possibly the most drastic adaptation Pieracci makes in the legendary account is his reduction in personages. Francesco is, of course, already dead, and the only Cenci present is Beatrice. The neoclassical, Alfierian model suggests that reduction of this kind, as in other narrowings of scope, makes for greater dramatic concentration and intensity. Shelley keeps Francesco alive into the fourth act and also puts on the stage in addition to Beatrice her stepmother Lucretia, and her brothers, Giacomo and Bernardo. This allows him greater dramatic complexity of characterization and irony and a greater number of tense scenes, some of the same qualities we prize in Shakespeare.

Pope Clement VIII made the forever unpopular judgment of sending Beatrice as well as her stepmother and brother to execution. Evidently wishing not to open old religious wounds, Pieracci refers to the final judge as the "Sovereign" or, at most, "holy old man," never by name. Another judge, Marsilio, screens for him. Shelley, on the other hand, gives as full play to his aversion for the Church as aesthetic considerations would allow him. He calls the Pope by his family name, in the singular number, Aldobrandino; he makes him self-serving in fining Francesco and implacable in sending the family to their death. Shelley's Francesco is a typical Italian Catholic, whose religion, Shelley tells us in the Preface, is "a passion, a persuasion, an excuse, a refuge; never a check" (p. 277). A tricky priest, Orsino, is a prime mover in the murder.

As compared with Shelley, Pieracci has little religious phraseology. Beatrice several times, especially at the end of Pieracci's play, invokes the physical symbols of the faith: significant weather phenomena, the altar, the shapeless form at creation, creation itself.[27] Ippolito, Marzio, and the male servants have at least one such reference each. Marsilio, the judge, twice refers to the doctrine of original sin.[28] Shelley's Francesco and Beatrice both frequently call on the power of heaven for their side, Francesco with far more certainty of favor than Beatrice is able to muster, though she is certain of the justice of her cause whether heaven aids or not. Since both Francesco and God are fathers, Cenci is certain God will honor his curse of Beatrice. The physical symbols of the faith are much on Francesco's lips; whereas Beatrice connects her father and his works with hell. As the end approaches she several times questions the justice of God and the validity of hope in Him. Francesco's curse is not his only violent appeal to heaven; he calls Lucretia a "blaspheming liar" and a "blaspheming" "palterer."[29] In sum, both Pieracci and Shelley treat religious phraseology exactly as we should expect them to do from evidence in the paragraph above: Pieracci avoids religious phraseology as he avoids the Pope. Shelley's Francesco speaks often in religious phraseology, in such a way as to remain the Italian Catholic of the Preface. We may add that Beatrice's uncertainty of providence well suits Shelley's own views.

The Alfierian model calls for much moralizing, and Pieracci has a great deal of this. As often as not this is expressed in commonplace observations about human life:[30] death takes every-

---

[27]The *Beatrice Cenci* is divided into acts and scenes but has no line numbers. The page numbers here and following are those of this publication: I, ii, p. 56; V, v, p. 88; V, v, p. 90; V, v, p. 90.

[28]II, ii, p. 62; IV, iii, p. 76.

[29]II, i, 162; IV, i, 73–74.

[30]In the "Scope of the Author" prefatory to his 1816 volume, Pieracci speaks of "maxims" and "expressions" graded to the "degree" of the tragedy and its characters. The *Beatrice Cenci* is a tragedy of only the second, or domestic, degree; hence, presumably, the commonplace moralizing.

one's beloved (I, i, p. 54); time conquers both happy and unhappy memories (I, i, p. 54); cunning teaches the concealment of crime (I, ii, p. 57); mirth in countenance indicates no war in the heart (II, vi, p. 65); the soul reacts to guilt with a shudder (II, viii, p. 66); heaven has the unworthy caught by snares (IV, i, p. 75); guilt does not reap happiness (IV, iii, p. 81); and so on. Some of the observations are stoic: bitter circumstances distinguish spirits (II, i, p. 61); constancy overcomes enemy fate (II, i, p. 61); the cowardly and the guilty flee, not the lover of honor (III, iii, p. 69); valor conquers fate and insults, restores innocence (III, v, p. 74); and the like. A pessimistic tone marks some of the commonplaces: some are born to misfortune (I, i, p. 55); time consumes us to dust (III, iii, p. 69); error ages us; good is a dream (III, iii, p. 69).

Shelley has few gnomic passages, and they are filled with the irony of life: others' estimate of us leads to our ill deeds (II, ii, 108–19); to prosper best, flatter the dark spirit of others (II, ii, 157–61); if only avenging remorse would warn us *before* the crime (V, i, 2–4); the crowd judges by what seems (V, i, 87–88); and his wrong to me is the basis of my being accused (V, ii, 130). Shelley has no interest in commonplaces; contrary to Keats's estimate of him, he does load every rift with ore.

The differences between the two plays have been set forth at some length before beginning on the evidence connecting them. This is done for two reasons: 1) to keep the account in balance; 2) to demonstrate the workings of two very different creative minds to the extent that divergent evidence is capable of doing this. In what follows, the readily recognizable parallels between Pieracci and Shelley, Shelley will use the materials to be found in Pieracci in his own individual way.

Of the likely contributions of Pieracci to Shelley, perhaps the one that strikes with most immediate impact is the character of Cammillo in Pieracci, "Camillo" in Shelley. There is no character of that name in the historical or known legendary accounts of the Cenci, including Es. Nor is there a Cammillo Farnese in the annals of the time, though the family of the Dukes of Parma were notable. He is a fiction, as earlier scholarship has acknowledged,[31]

---

[31]Bates, p. 69; Curran, p. 44.

but he is the invention of Pieracci, not Shelley, to be the ineffectual pleader on Beatrice's behalf, to be also, with Ippolitio, a
French-type confidant and a Greek chorus of the Alfierian drama.
Shelley understandably drops the neoclassical and classical aspects of Cammillo/Camilo, and, following his practice in other
parts of the play of involving the church, makes him a cardinal as
well as a nephew and collection agency — a Pardoner — of the Pope
(I, i, 1–14; V, iv, 24), who as the historical Clement VIII had two
very influential cardinal nephews. Also Shelley had to give him
high rank; otherwise he could not perform the function Shelley
needed, as intermediary between Cenci and the Pope and between
Beatrice and the Pope. Shelley keeps Camillo essentially in his
Pieracci role as ineffectual pleader, and his sudden failure as
pleader heightens the tension of the last scene, perhaps the principal reason Shelley the playwright seized upon him when he
found him in Pieracci. Shelley is making creative use of Pieracci
materials not to be found in his manuscript source. That two
playwrights working in the same story a few years apart should
independently invent a similar character with a similar name
seems beyond the stretch of reasonable probability. Cammillo/
Camillo must be considered as two parallels, one for his name and
one for his function.[32]

---

[32]How many male Italian first names are there? To cover as nearly as possible
the use of such names during the time of Pieracci and Shelley, the author went
through a ten-volume biographical dictionary of Italians illustrious in science,
letters, and arts during the eighteenth century and most of the first half of the
nineteenth century [Emilio De Tipaldo, ed., *Biografia degli Italiani Illustri nelle
Scienze, Lettere ed Arti del Secolo XVIII, e de' Contemporanei Compilata da
Letterati Italiani di Ogni Provincia* (Venezia: Alvisopoli, 1834–1845), 10 vols.],
and found a total of 249 male Italian first names. On this basis the statistical
chances that Shelley thought of the name Camillo independently of any source are
one in 249. The total number of appearances of all male Italian first names, not all
different, in the ten volumes is 1,354, which divided by the eight appearances of
Camillo leaves 169. On this basis the chances of Shelley's independent invention
are one in 169.

Under the rules of probability, the fact that Camillo/Cammillo plays a
similar role in both plays *multiplies* the improbability that Shelley independently
invented the name and character. The best way to factor him in his parallel role in
both plays as ineffectual pleader who tries to save Beatrice is to borrow from the
famous "twenty-questions" game, awarding a factor of two at each stage. (1) Is the
person male or female? Male. (2) Is he young or old? Old or comparatively so. (3)
Is he friendly or hostile? Friendly. (4) Is he a passive comforter or intervener?

In all but one of the seven legendary accounts of the Cenci murder studied by Professor Steffan, the Pope weighed the crimes of the father against those of the children in possible extenuation of their guilt.[33] In the other, Es, he was for a time favorably impressed by a similar weighing in the documents of the advocate Farinacci (pp. 409–10). Neither Pieracci nor Shelley gives the Sovereign/Pope any such temporary bias. Though the Sovereign appears to be more than sympathetic in Pieracci, his early reaction as reported by Ippolito does not include balancing off Cenci's crimes against his violent death (III, iii, p. 69); and Shelley's Pope, with the crime of Paolo Santa Croce before him, refuses to do so (V, iv, 15–24). Both wish to make an example of the guilty.

There is nothing in Es of Beatrice's denying at the trial any acquaintance with the murderer or murderers[34] that implicate her, as both Pieracci's and Shelley's Beatrice do (P. IV, iii, p. 77; S. V, ii, 20–23). Pieracci's intent seems to be to confuse the issue of guilt, Shelley's to point up Beatrice's valiant attempt to escape.

There is no evidence in Es that the Roman street crowd that pressed about the Cenci as they went to their execution were "vain and senseless," as Shelley's Beatrice forebodes, or that they cast on the doomed "curses or faded pity" (V, iii, 36, 41). Historically it was quite the contrary; the curses were for the Pope. But Pieracci, anticipating Shelley, early rings Beatrice about with reports of a clamorous mob. They shout her name, demand to see her, call her guilty.[35] Pieracci makes this change and the one immediately above to heighten the tensions enveloping his heroine, and Shelley accepts both changes, apparently to deepen the emotional

Intervener. (5) Is his intervention violent or by persuasive means? By persuasive means. With this factor of ten, the chances of Shelley's arriving at the name and role of Camillo independently of Pieracci are, by multiplying the first number for the name, 249, by 10, one in 2,490. Similarly, if we multiply the second number, 169, by 10, the chances are one in 1,690. At the same time, the chances for the supplying of the name and role of Camillo by any other source drop virtually to zero. Of course, it must be stated that what we have here is a high order of probability; it is not the same thing as proof.

[33]Steffan, p. 616.

[34]Pieracci has both Olimpio and Marzio alive and present at the trial; Shelley stands closer to Es in having Olimpio already slain at that time.

[35]II, vi, p. 65; II, vii, p. 66; II, viii, p. 66.

plight of Beatrice just before her rise to a noble acceptance of her fate.

Another parallel in the two playwrights that Shelley could not have obtained from Es is Beatrice's sense of the continuing evil power of her father even after his death. Pieracci's Beatrice says, "I feel consumed within myself. . . . A superior force invades me. Before my eyes I see everything change. . . . Tyrannous furies, wickedness, of which there is no equal, conspire to my damage" (III, iv, pp. 70–71). A little later in the same scene she says, "[My father] was the tyrant of his days. His evil genius has not died out yet" (III, iv, p. 72). Even after her trial and acquittal she feels his presence: "A terrible ghost holds my feet and heart in chains: I cannot leave Rome" (IV, iv, p. 82). Shelley's Beatrice intensifies all this in one speech: "For was he not alone omnipotent/ On Earth, and ever present? Even though dead,/ Does not his spirit live in all that breathe,/ And work for me and mine still the same ruin,/ Scorn, pain, despair?" (V, iv, 68–72). A subjective emphasis, sometimes hallucinatory, in Pieracci and especially Shelley, here and in imagery, and missing from the insistent narrative of Es, accounts for the invention by Pieracci and adoption by Shelley of such motifs as this, as well as the one which follows. The purpose in both playwrights is a tragic intensification of the inner life of the character and, consequently, a heightened tension for the play.

A parallel in both plays is the fact that guilty souls, or souls about to be guilty, feel the presence of retributive telltale objects in their environment. Once more subjective intensity builds dramatic intensity. Pieracci's Marzio tells the judge, Marsilio, "We had scarcely consummated the terrible misdeed than cruel remorse and fear were tormenting us. We saw written everywhere our horrible sentence; and we feared that everyone might know our crime. In this horrible, atrocious struggle of continual suffering we resolved to leave those walls where the blood still was coagulated, that blood that we had shed" (IV, iii, p. 81). Shelley also has telltale walls. As his Cenci contemplates his terrible intent against Beatrice, he tells departing Lucretia, "you know/ That savage rock, the Castle of Petrella:/ 'Tis safely walled, and moated round about:/ Its dungeons underground, and its thick towers/ Never told tales; though they have heard and seen/ What might

25

make dumb things speak." Then to himself: "The all-beholding sun yet shines; I hear/ A busy stir of men about the streets;/ I see the bright sky through the window panes:/ It is a garish, broad, and peering day;/ Loud, light, suspicious, full of eyes and ears" (II, i, 167-72, 174-78). These last two quotations serve to intensify both the telltale, developed above and found in Pieracci and Shelley, and the inanimate become sensate, to be treated later and found almost entirely in Shelley alone.

The next two parallels are concatenations of images about single themes, and these not only link the two plays in the same way as other parallels, but since they appear together and in "mad" scenes of the two plays, they also link the "mad" scenes, which become another parallel.

From the last scenes of Pieracci, where there are other creative stimuli for Shelley, Shelley seems to have derived a figure of speech for one of his earlier passages. Cammillo wishes to banish Beatrice's despair by a change of scene. "But where," says Beatrice, "could I show myself, I, a desperate woman, to snatch even from the flowers the grateful odor, to roil the most limpid wave, to poison the air you breathe?" (V, vi, p. 89). From this guilty source of pollution in Pieracci she becomes Beatrice polluted in Shelley, a result of her father's act. Once more Shelley reworks his raw materials to his own purposes. Since, as will soon be apparent, there are two figures to discuss in Beatrice's long speech at the beginning of Shelley's Act III, the whole of it is quoted here and not simply the eight lines carrying most of the figure of pollution from the *Beatrice Cenci*; those lines containing it are italicized (those underlined with a solid line are for the next figure):

> How comes this hair undone?
> Its wandering strings must be what blind me so,
> And yet I tied it fast.—O, horrible!
> The pavement sinks under my feet! The walls
> Spin round! I see a woman weeping there,
> And standing calm and motionless, whilst I
> Slide giddily as the world reels. . . . My God!
> The beautiful blue heaven is flecked with blood!
> The sunshine on the floor is black! The air

Is changed to vapours such as the dead breathe
In charnel pits! Pah! I am choked! *There creeps*
A clinging, black, contaminating mist
About me . . . 'tis substantial, heavy, thick,
I cannot pluck it from me, for it glues
My fingers and my limbs to one another,
And eats into my sinews, and dissolves
My flesh to a pollution, poisoning
The subtle, pure, and inmost spirit of life!
My God! I never knew what the mad felt
Before; for I am mad beyond all doubt!
(*More wildly.*) No, I am dead! These *putrefying limbs*
Shut round and sepulchre the panting soul
Which would burst forth into the wandering air!
   (*A pause.*)
What hideous thought was that I had even now?
'Tis gone; and yet its burthen remains here
O'er these dull eyes . . . upon this weary heart!
O, world! O, life! O, day! O, misery!
         (III, i, 6–32)

The pollution figure recurs more than once later in the same scene. "O blood, which art my father's blood," says Beatrice, "Circling through these contaminated veins,/ If thou, poured forth on the polluted earth,/ Could wash away the crime. . . ." (95–98). She calls her limbs "a foul den" (129–30), then in irony shifts the figure to her reputation: "ay, lay all bare/ So that my unpolluted fame should be . . . a stale mouthed story" (157–59). Shelley transfers the pollution from Pieracci's Beatrice, who is a polluting object of guilt-ridden self-abhorrence, to his own Beatrice, who is intense in her polluted victimization—a dramatic coup d'état made possible by Shelley's beginning the play with Cenci alive.

    The same long passage of Shelley contains another figure— a strange complex of sun, blackness, sky, and blood—that finds its parallel in the same character and scene of Pieracci as the pollution figure in this passage. A sentence or two after her words on herself as a pollutant, ending "to poison the air you breathe," Pieracci's Beatrice resumes, "The sun this morning rose so black, but a more fearful night will descend with anger and blood. . . . Nature takes revenge. . . ."—expressions not difficult to recognize behind lines 13 and 14 (marked above with underlining) of

Shelley's Beatrice: "The beautiful blue heaven is flecked with blood!/ The sunshine on the floor is black!" It would seem that this and the pollution figure adjacent in Pieracci went hand in hand from Pieracci into the same passage of Shelley. Both Pieracci and Shelley intensify the effect of what has happened—poison and rape—by Beatrice's projection into externals of her "mad," to some extent hallucinatory, inner state.

When we remember that the passage from Shelley quoted at length is at the heart of Beatrice's so-called mad scene, we realize a new dimension. The star system of the contemporary English stage, as projected in the acting of Edmund Kean and Eliza O'Neill, has been cited for its effect upon the action and characterization of *The Cenci*. Shelley had witnessed Miss O'Neill as Bianca in Henry Hart Milman's *Fazio*—a role which she played with the screams, pathos, and drawn-out insensibility that were her specialties.[36] There is evidence that Shelley had her in mind for the part of Beatrice as he wrote,[37] and the mad speech of Act III has seemed made to order for her. Distraction on the stage was, of course, not the exclusive property of the English theatre. Pieracci's Beatrice climaxes an Alfierian and contemporary Italian gamut of passion and tears with two last mad speeches as she stands tottering on the stage and slowly dying of poison. We have two figures of considerable compass or complexity tying them to Beatrice's mad speeches of Shelley's Act III, Scene i. These are the last words of Pieracci's Beatrice, punctuated as above by the ellipses of incoherence: "Heaven shows a happy look . . . the air is becoming more beautiful. . . . Who would believe it? . . . Even the shapeless mass. . . . The whole creation rejoices at my death." This is not to deny the connection with Eliza O'Neill and the English star system, which I think is sound, but we should add that Shelley seems to have drawn substance and a touchstone for his mode from an Italian dramatic scene. All these his imagination rewrought to his poetic and dramatic intent.

The section above on what in Pieracci is clearly not Shel-

[36]Joseph W. Donohue, Jr., "Shelley's Beatrice and the Romantic Concept of Tragic Character," *KSJ*, 17 (1968), 53, 56–59; Curran, pp. 158, n. 2; 168–71.

[37]Donohue, p. 60; Curran, 170–71.

leyan source treats 1) Pieracci's much greater compression of time, including his use of unity of time; 2) Pieracci's unity of place; 3) his reduction of attempts on Francesco's life to one; 4) his reduction in personages, including his reduction of living Cencis to one, Beatrice; 5) his almost complete deletion of the Pope; 6) his small use of religious phraseology; and 7) his great use of commonplace moralizing in contrast to Shelley's few gnomic but ironical passages.

The next section, on what in Pieracci seems clearly related to Shelley's work and not to be found in Es, treats 1) the name of Cammillo/Camilo in both playwrights; 2) his function; 3) the Sovereign's desire to make an example of the guilty, and his not balancing off the crimes of Francesco against his murder; 4) Beatrice's denial in both playwrights of acquaintance with the murderer or murderers; 5) the hostility of the general public toward Beatrice; 6) the sense of the continuing evil power of Francesco after his death; 7) the sense of surrounding, retributive, telltale objects; 8) a complex figure combining sun, blackness, sky, and blood; 9) in combination with #8 in both playwrights, a figure in which Beatrice appears to be polluting or polluted; and 10) a mad scene involving Beatrice in both playwrights in which appears a nexus of #s 8 and 9.

In addition, there are certain facts and inclinations not in Es that both playwrights have in common; and since, as Rogers says, Shelley recreates and makes his own his source materials, differences in the instances that follow make it difficult to determine that he does or does not derive them from Pieracci.

Pieracci and Shelley generally reduce, sometimes eliminate, the sordid, the abnormal, and the violent in the old account.[38] Shelley says in his Preface, "The person who would treat such a subject must increase the ideal, and diminish the actual horror of the events, so that the pleasure which arises from the poetry which exists in these tempestuous sufferings and crimes may mitigate the pain of the contemplation of the moral depravity from which they spring." (p. 276). He once told Trelawny that the original events

---

[38]Smith, p. 80, has made this observation about Shelley's play.

were "far more horrible than I have painted them."[39]

Much of the sordid and abnormal in Es and other legendary accounts neither Pieracci nor Shelley has—Cenci's male sodomy and attempts at persuasive incest with Beatrice—; and their not having these should be treated here as part of a broader similar intent on the part of both playwrights. Whether or not he knew this source, Pieracci is much less specific than Es in charging Francesco with heterosexual antics (with the "girls . . . and common courtezans" of Es), and Shelley omits them altogether.

Of course, Pieracci wishes to preserve the decorum of his play and the tragic dignity of his heroine as well as to reduce as much as possible her provocation to homicide, hence reducing her probable involvement. Shelley, on his side, drops the charge of sodomy against Francesco for the theatrically more acceptable one of murder, and reserves his assault on theatre convention for Francesco's incestuous rape of Beatrice, masking it in "delicacy."[40] Like Pieracci he wants as far as possible to exculpate his heroine,[41] but by the opposite tactic of aggravating Cenci's villainy and

---

[39]Edward John Trelawny, *Recollections of the Last Days of Shelley and Byron* in *The Life of Percy Bysshe Shelley* (New York: E. P. Dutton and Co., 1913), p. 198; Curran, p. 42.

[40]Shelley raised the question in a letter to Peacock of about July 20, 1819: "my principal doubt as to whether it [*The Cenci*] would succeed as an acting play hangs entirely on the question as to whether any such a thing as incest in this shape however treated wd. be admitted on the stage—I think however it will form no objection, considering first that the facts are matter of history, & secondly the peculiar delicacy with which I have treated it—," *Letters*, II, 102. In another letter to Peacock on September 9, he bases some hopes on the fact that " 'Oedipus' is performed on the fastidious French stage, a play much more broad than this," *Letters*, II, 118–19. A letter to Leigh Hunt of May 24, 1820, expresses some impatience with objectors: "Bessy tells me that people reprobate the subject of my tragedy—let them abase Sophocles, Massinger, Voltaire & Alfieri in the same sentence, & I am content.—I maintain that my scenes are as delicate & free from offence as theirs," *Letters*, II, 200.

[41]Smith has Shelley both attracted and repelled by the story and its heroine, and the repulsion is especially apparent in the rough draft of the Preface [*Note Books* II, 89, n.]. By reducing the horrible in the account, Shelley, says Smith, effects "a partial justification of the heroine" (p. 82). In the Preface (p. 276) Shelley says that Beatrice's fault lay in her taking revenge for her wrongs instead of trying to "convert the injurer" "by peace and love." Nevertheless, as this writing shows, he also effects "partial justification" by aggravating her wrongs and, hence, provocation.

Beatrice's provocation to homicide. Shelley omits Francesco's heterosexual antics, possibly to avoid complicating the character of Lucretia, Cenci's wife and Beatrice's stepmother, whom he has wished to subordinate to Beatrice. Thus, both playwrights eliminate undesirable action for two purposes: 1) to exculpate their heroine as far as possible, with an opposite dramatic strategy; 2) to avoid alienating their public by unacceptable sins on Francesco's part and too much gore in his taking off. Pieracci makes his reductions for neoclassical decorum. Both must reveal or not reveal with some delicacy. Since Shelley's dramatic strategy requires much more violence, or revealed violence, than Pieracci's he must exercise much greater delicacy, to keep, as he says, the ideal predominant over horror, the pleasure of poetry predominant over the pain of moral depravity.

Both playwrights resemble Es in having Cenci place Beatrice in solitary confinement but diverge on the beatings administered there in Es (p. 401). In Pieracci the blows fall instead on the servants (IV, iii, p. 76); whereas in Shelley they fall on Beatrice with such added brutality as nakedness, dampness, haling by the hair, trampling, starvation, reptiles, and strange food and drink (II, i, 64–71; III, i, 43–48). Pieracci evidently wishes to make Olimpio and Marzio more independent of Beatrice in their resolve to murder and, as well, to preserve the tragic dignity of his heroine. Shelley wishes by the added brutality, as in other matters, to enhance Beatrice's motivation for her part in the murder. To the same intent he invents Cenci's self-proclaimed sadism (I, i, 77–117). Pieracci has no need of such enhancement since he never makes clear Beatrice's part in the murder.

As we turn to the more sanguinary details of the story, where mitigation seems called for if anywhere, we find that both Pieracci and Shelley do indeed sponge away a great deal of the gore of Es. The similarities here are rather in structural decision than in detail. In Pieracci, Cenci is murdered by stabbing (IV, iii, p. 79), not by having a nail driven into his brain via his eye and another into his neck as in Es (p. 405). In addition to reducing the gore this allows the wounds to be counted to the possible exculpation of Beatrice. There is nowhere in the play mention of torture to induce confession, and though the death penalty awaits Olimpio and Marzio, no specific form of execution is mentioned. Beatrice is not condemned but exonerated; and she chooses what is probably the mildest form of self-administered death, by poison. The judge, Marsilio, and the captain of the militia, Fausto,[42] nearly always outdo each other in expressions of sympathy for her. The brutal closing scenes of Es, which spare few details of the scaffold and quote the very words of Beatrice as her head departs from her trunk, are not for Pieracci as Beatrice stands, somewhat unsteadily but in noble self-sacrifice, at the curtain. The last words of Marsilio (V, vi, p. 89) suggest that Beatrice's plea for Olimpio and Marzio earlier in this last scene has not gone unheeded and they will be spared.

Shelley's characters mention stabbing, but Francesco Cenci is finally dispatched bloodlessly, by strangulation. As in Es, Marzio, Giacomo, and Lucretia submit to torture (offstage) and confess. Beatrice also follows the scenario of Es in making her ambiguous confession under the pleas of the other Cenci (except Bernardo) and the threat of torture, though the bonds of torture, applied in Es, are nowhere in evidence. There is mention of the Cenci's being doomed to be dragged by horses (V, iii, 34–36) as the Pope had at first considered in Es (p. 408), but they are actually to be executed by decapitation. Bernardo is not prosecuted, threatened with death, and finally spared at the cost of watching the others executed as in Es; and the special brutality dealt out to Giacomo in Es does not appear to be in prospect. Shelley's Beatrice, like Pieracci's, is still alive at the curtain, though on her way to death. Pieracci and Shelley both discard the excess blood of the Cenci legend.

Ever since the sixteenth century Italians have loved Beatrice. Pieracci has shared this love and appealed to it in his public. All his life Shelley engaged in what Rogers calls Ariadne quests; he rescued his first-wife-to-be, Harriet Westbrook, from her claimed oppression and wished to rescue Emilia Viviani, whose parents had confined her to a convent. Beatrice's story as he found it and

---

[42]For an exception, in II, vii, p. 66, Fausto looking at Beatrice says, "She sighs; oh late repentance!"

her supposed portrait awakened the powerful emotion he records in the Preface to *The Cenci* (p. 278). With the same interest in Beatrice, Pieracci and Shelley pursue opposite paths. Pieracci keeps vague the evil deeds Cenci does to Beatrice or in her presence in order to have the burden of homicidal provocation fall on others, the servants. As the play ends it is not certain, in spite of her suicide, what part if any she had in the murder: this is Pieracci's method of exculpation. Shelley lessens but preserves her part in the murder; he exculpates her as best he can by distributing the guilt among all participants and by vastly increasing and bringing out Cenci's evil deeds to her, including incestuous rape, thus increasing her homicidal provocation and diminishing her guilt. Neither Pieracci nor Shelley mentions Cenci's attempt at persuasive incest with Beatrice to be found in the Italian source, Es. Each playwright has pursued his love of Beatrice with a greatly different plan.

Both Pieracci and Shelley reduce Beatrice's role in the murder.[43] In this matter as some others, Shelley takes a compromise position between Es and Pieracci. Since Shelley does not follow Pieracci's manner at its ingenious best in advocacy of Beatrice, let us compare Es and Shelley first. In Es the notion of murder first occurs to Beatrice and Lucretia. The friend, Guerra, hears, approves, and promises help. Giacomo, Beatrice's brother, is then drawn into the plot by Beatrice (pp. 402–03). In Shelley Cenci first suggests his own murder by accusing Lucretia of harboring the intent (II, i, 139–48). Giacomo next stops just short of clarifying a hint of murder for Orsino's receptive ears, and Orsino in a soliloquy approves for reasons of his own (II, ii, 72–74, 120–22). After the rape Beatrice wildly utters the word "parricide" as a figure of speech: "Like Parricide . . . / Misery has killed its father" (III, i, 36–37). Orsino, who is Guerra renamed and reshaped to carry a great deal of the Es Beatrice's burden of guilt,[44] makes the

---

[43]Smith, p. 81, with Es and the Note Book Memorandum before him, says Shelley's Beatrice is "transformed from an active to a more passive participant in the crime."

[44]Ibid. Joan Rees, "Shelley's Orsino: Evil in 'The Cenci'," *KSMB*, 12 (1961), 3, sees Orsino as one of "the two principal agents of evil in the play." Charles L.

first open suggestion of murder; and both Beatrice and Lucretia join him in a murder pact (III, i, 219–33). Orsino is then the link as Giacomo joins the pact, having independently pursued his own earlier thought (III, i, 340–41). Thus Shelley distributes the burden of the initiative, making it arise in five minds and not simply one or two. In the actual murder that follows, Shelley's diminishing of Beatrice's role from her role in Es consists principally in her surrendering the initiative in the plotting to Orsino, her not entering the murder bedroom, and her having nothing to do with the disposal of the body. Now for a look at Pieracci.

All that we ever come to know of the plotting and committing of the murder in Pieracci emerges in the testimony of Olimpio and Marzio before the judge, Marsilio, and in the presence of Beatrice. If Shelley distributes the blame and, so, diminishes Beatrice's role by a clear management of plot-and-character line, Pieracci comes to the same end by making the testimony of Olimpio and Marzio so contradictory in every way—internally as between one and the other, in one instance with external evidence, and with the few words of Beatrice—that we never can be sure what part if any Beatrice had in the crime. Olimpio never gets an opportunity to testify in the other versions; in Es he is murdered by Guerra's hired assassins (p. 406), and in Shelley's fidelity of a sort to Es he falls "desperately fighting" the Pope's officers immediately after the crime (IV, iv, 86–87). It is clear why Pieracci kept him alive: to add to the confusion and contradiction he needed to preserve his heroine's stature.

Olimpio testifies that Beatrice persuaded them to do the murder and gave them the knife. On the contrary, Marzio says that the knife was his own and not supplied by Beatrice. She, for her part, denies acquaintance with Olimpio and Marzio (IV, iii, p. 77). Olimpio says she was at the scene and screamed "strike!" When the two men lost heart, she incited them and they killed Cenci with three stabs. Then she stabbed the body. Marsilio consults an autopsy report and says there were only three stab

---

Adams, "The Structure of *The Cenci*," *Drama Survey*, 4 (1965), 147, sees Shelley "presenting an Iago-like Orsino to initiate action, control pace, and present a separate kind of evil."

wounds in the body. Marzio now doubles the contradiction by saying Beatrice did not stab the body (IV, iii, p. 79). He adds, however, that Beatrice gave him her father's mantle, which he shows, as part of his reward for the murder. Beatrice says anyone capable of murdering her father would be capable of taking the mantle for himself (IV, iii, p. 80).

Seeing that their case is hopeless, Marzio says, "let us try to save Beatrice." He and Olimpio did the deed, he says, in revenge for ill treatment. Beatrice was their idol and not guilty. After the murder he and Olimpio fled in remorse and fear. Trembling and fearful though he is, Marzio has risen above his fate in self-sacrifice, somewhat in advance of Beatrice's doing so and three years in advance of his doing similarly in Shelley's play. The means are different, but both playwrights reduce Beatrice's role in the murder.

Pieracci is turning a neat trick. He presents the facts of a sordid murder case substantially as they are in the legend, but he so beclouds the issue of who did what as to bring out practically everybody a hero.

After the crime the historical Beatrice Cenci wrote a petition to the Pope. With their usual tendency to favor her, the legendary accounts, including Es, have the petition antedating the crime, and both playwrights, of course, adopt this. It credits her with a desperate attempt to avoid the crime, and puts some of the blame on papal insensivity. Es has the document "afterwards found among the collection of memorials, and it is pretended that it never came before the Pope" (p. 402). Pieracci gives the Sovereign, as he calls him, the benefit of the doubt, and has the petition deliberately withheld, by Aldobrando, the friend of Beatrice's father (III, iv, pp. 71–72). Whatever the temptation to follow the thrust of Es and add one more stroke of insensitivity to the Pope's character, Shelley also has the petition deliberately withheld, by the priest Orsino, who thus acquires one more stroke of a deeper guilt, treachery, similar to Aldobrando's (I, ii, 68–71); he has already sufficiently loaded Cenci with guilt.

For a similar reason Shelley makes another change similar to one originating in Pieracci. Pieracci has Beatrice expressing her early dismay when she asks whether heaven did not thunder upon the wicked hands exhuming Francesco's body (I, ii, p. 56). The noble isolation of her self-sacrifice comes forth in almost her last words as she stands dying, when she marvels that "Heaven shows a happy look" at her death (V, vi, p. 90). Similarly, among the differences from Es noted in Shelley by previous scholarship is Beatrice's momentary doubt about the goodness of God: "You do well telling me to trust in God,/ I hope I do trust in Him. In whom else/ Can any trust? And yet my heart is cold."[45] This, in the last scene, is part of her descent into despair just before her rise into acceptance of her fate. Shelley has very possibly adapted Pieracci's material to his own craft of tragic drama.

Pieracci's Fausto asks skeptically, "Where is there fear without crime?" and Beatrice replies, "There are souls whose innocence cannot keep fear, often fatal, from entering" (I, iii, p. 58). In other words, the fear aroused by accusation may fasten on an innocent person a look of guilt or an inability to defend himself that may lead to his being convicted. In a similar concept, without authorization from Es, Shelley has Beatrice interpreting her mother's fainting in the metaphors that power grips the victim in fear, and its look produces the appearance of guilt: "She fears that power is as a beast which grasps/ And loosens not: a snake whose look transmutes/ All things to guilt which is its nutriment" (IV, iv, 178–80). Shelley fortifies the image that appears in Pieracci with a basilisk image and uses it to heighten, by Beatrice's minimizing the physical act of Lucretia's fainting, the arrest scene that envelops it. There is a fair possiblity that Shelley drew upon Pieracci here.

Both playwrights employ a great deal of imagery for the external projection of inner states. In the Preface to *Prometheus Unbound*, Shelley makes a statement about his imagery in that work which applies with equal force to *The Cenci*, written at the same time: "The imagery which I have employed will be found, in many instances, to have been drawn from the operations of the human mind, or from those external actions by which they are expressed" (p. 205). Shelley's purpose becomes clear in the Preface to *The Cenci*, in which he says that the imagery in the play

---

[45]Steffan, p. 607, n. 13; S. V, iv, 87–89.

must be "employed in the illustration of strong feeling" (p. 277). The same statements could apply to much of Pieracci's imagery, but his imagery is different from Shelley's in intent and form. Pieracci's imagery constantly reminds us that Cenci is already dead when the play opens. At the center of Pieracci's image is a conventional, emotionally-toned word figuratively involved in physical action coming as an *aftereffect* of earlier dramatic action. The heart, for example, offers depths to plumb, space to pour torrents into which become stone tears; it harbors motions of fear, it shifts from moment to moment, it dissolves into tears, it is invaded by fear, it is besieged by emotions, it is held in chains by a terrible ghost, it is drowned in tears. Loss of honor would weave calamity about the heart.[46] Other key words for imagery in Pieracci are tears, fear, anguish, honor, hope, guilt, cruelty, soul, horror, virtue, and desire[47] —generally reflective of neoclassical major action in retrospect.

Shelley's "external actions" by which "operations of the human mind" "are expressed" heighten intensity by *anticipating* dramatic action; they heighten threatening danger or death— first, the death of Cenci, then of Beatrice. Orsino feels Beatrice's eyes anatomizing him nerve by nerve (I, ii, 83–87), Lucretia sees Beatrice's eyes shooting forth "a wandering and strange spirit" (III, i, 81–82). Cenci will see to it that "her stubborn will . . . shall stoop . . . low" (IV, i, 10–11). He is, says Lucretia, one who "walks . . . / Through crimes" (IV, i, 16–17). Suspecting the priest of treachery, Giacomo threatens Orsino: "Let the sword speak what the indignant tongue/ Disdains to brand thee with" (V, i, 55–56). Death figures are frequent, and always before the fact. Giacomo pictures his father sinking "into the white and yellow spasms of

---

[46]I, iii, p. 58; II, i, p. 61; II, vi, p. 65; II, viii, p. 66; III, iv, p. 73; IV, iii, p. 79; IV, iv, p. 82; IV, iv, p. 82; V, iv, p. 86; III, iv, p. 71.

[47]Heart is covered above in n. 46. Tears: I, i, p. 54; II, i, p. 61; II, vi, p. 65; III, iv, p. 73; V, iv, p. 86. Fear: II, vi, p. 64; IV, iii, p. 79. Anguish: I, iii, p. 58; II, i, p. 61; II, i, p. 61; III, iii, p. 69; V, iv, p. 86. Honor: II, i, p. 61; III, iii, p. 69; III, iv, p. 71; V, iv, p. 86. Hope: II, iv, p. 63; III, iii, p. 69. Guilt: II, vi, p. 65; II, viii, p. 66; III, iv, p. 71; IV, iii, p. 78; V, iv, p. 82. Cruelty: II, vi, p. 64; II, vi, p. 65. Soul: II, viii, p. 66; III, iv, p. 71; IV, iii, p. 77; IV, iii, p. 81; V, iv, p. 87. Horror: III, iv, p. 70. Virtue: III, iii, p. 69; III, iv, p. 73. Desire: IV, iii, p. 81. The above list is not exhaustive.

death" (III, ii, 20–21). In a figure reminiscent of *Othello*, Giacomo relights the lamp with "I cannot thus relume/ My father's life" (III, ii, 51–52). Cenci threatens to make Bernardo's "youth/ The sepulchre of hope" (IV, i, 52–53). Beatrice sees herself as one of the *morituri* decked out as though dead: "Shall the light multitude/ Fling, at their choice, curses or faded pity,/ Sad funeral flowers to deck a living corpse,/ Upon us?" (V, iii, 40–43). Death appears to her in the same all-too-realistic figure as it does to Claudio in *Measure for Measure*: "So young to go/ Under the obscure, cold, rotting, wormy ground" (V, iv, 49–50). Hope, she finds, is the worst suffering of all: it can "find place/ Upon the giddy, sharp and narrow hour/ Tottering beneath us" (V, iv, 99–101).

The heroines in both plays experience hallucinations in their mad scenes, but there is little counterpart in Pieracci for the hallucinatory response Shelley's Cenci projects into his physical surroundings, giving them sensate life: "O, thou most silent air, that shalt not hear/ What now I think! Thou, pavement, which I tread/ Towards her chamber, —let your echoes talk of my imperious step" (I, i, 140–43). To Lucretia: "But I will take you where you may persuade/ The stones you tread on to deliver you" (II, i, 163–64). Nature is knowledgeable: "The all-beholding sun yet shines . . . / It is a garish, broad, and peering day;/ Loud, light, suspicious, full of eyes and ears" (II, i, 174, 177–78). The only counterpart in Pieracci seems to be in Beatrice's last words, in which she has the whole creation rejoicing in her death. There is little counterpart in Pieracci for the response Shelley's Cenci projects into the physical, but we have seen earlier in both playwrights the response of characters to telltale objects in their environment.

Shelley's Orsino says of the Cenci's tendency to "self-anatomy," " 'tis a trick of this same family/ To analyse their own and other minds" (II, ii, 108–10), and this "trick" is in evidence throughout the play. The effect of Pieracci's *Beatrice Cenci* seems more likely here than it does with the outward, physical projection of inner states. Here the words express only inner states. As the only Cenci present, Pieracci's Beatrice is constantly explaining herself to the willing and sympathetic audience of Cammillo, Ippolito, Marsilio, Fausto, and the servants. Such explanations account for most of the action in this slow-moving play, which often seems the outward projection of an internal debate by the principal character, who captures even more the focus of the play than does Shelley's heroine. Beatrice experiences a loss of orientation in the mad scenes of both plays. Shelley draws imagery from the operations of other minds besides Beatrice's, showing their probing of the psychological states that grip them. Giacomo expresses to Orsino the horror of an intent that struggles just outside verbal formulation: "we trust/ Imagination with such phantasies/ As the tongue dares not fashion into words,/ Which have no words, their horror makes them dim/ To the mind's eye" (II, ii, 83–87). Then Giacomo carries away a psyche divided against itself: "Pardon me, that I say farewell—farewell!/ I would that to my own suspected self/ I could address a word so full of peace" (II, ii, 101–03). Orsino also is given to "self-anatomy." In his turn he confesses to himself his enthrallment to sexual fantasies: "I clasp the phantom of unfelt delights/ Till weak imagination half possesses/ The self-created shadow" (II, ii, 141–43). After the murder unexpected remorse seizes him: "where shall I/ Find the disguise to hide me from myself,/ As now I skulk from every other eye?" (V, i, 102–04). We have discovered in analysis of these two plays that inner intensity of characters, whether projected outward into physical objects or not, is used to intensify characterization and the entire atmosphere of the play.

The heroine is alive as the curtain falls in both plays, a fact to be commented upon below, but their leave-taking is very different. Pieracci's Beatrice has taken upon herself sole responsibility for the murder. She stands tottering and partly incoherent from her self-administered poison, seeing the whole creation rejoicing at her death. Shelley stays closer to the legend. With her enigmatic confession behind her, his Beatrice has nobly risen to her fate for an Aristotelian and Shakespearean catharsis as she and Lucretia bind up each other's hair for the headsman's ax.

However different the deaths of the two Beatrices are to be, a similar intent of the two playwrights should be noted. Es, Shelley's source, spares no details of the scaffold scene, but in both plays Beatrice, albeit soon to die, is still alive at the curtain. One could argue that each playwright could arrive independently at the same ending for dramaturgical reasons, since the last words and acts of a tragic hero acquire a poignancy all their own as he rises to a noble acceptance of his fate ("Nothing in his life became him like the leaving it"), and effect for the audience a catharsis of pity and fear. Shakespeare, to be sure, sometimes supplies a calm space of reconciliation after the death in which some such new action takes place as provision for the succession. Neither Pieracci nor Shelley envisions a reconciliation. Pieracci came to this final scene first, and suggestion here adds cumulatively to its power in other similarities between the two plays.

As the end of Pieracci's play approaches, Beatrice is enmeshed in a web of dilemmas in honor that would have warmed Corneille's heart. Earlier she has refused Cammillo's offers to use his influence in her behalf and to escort her from the country; her sorrowful distress cannot be left behind her (I, i, p. 55). Nor, as the trap of the law closes about her, will she leave by the back gate with Ippolito; she would sacrifice her honor, which she values more than life (III, iii, p. 69). Judge Marsilio sets up the final dilemma by exonerating her. Will she let Olimpio and Marzio pay with their lives, one of them leaving behind an old, destitute mother? No, she will assume the whole guilt, without going into detail, and pay the whole price. Under the circumstances, who can fault a reader who decides her suicide pays a debt of honor only, and she had no part in the murder? Pieracci probably expected the ardent admirers of Beatrice to thank him in a body. She has come a long way from the sensual heroine of history, who seems to have had an affair with Olimpio, possibly an illegitimate child, who even in the generally sympathetic account of Es was the chief driving force in a murder plot.

There is a reason for treating at length Pieracci's exculpation of Beatrice by contrived ambiguity. One critic, referring to the passage in Shelley's Preface, "It is in the restless and anatomizing casuistry with which men seek the justification of Beatrice, yet feel that she had done what needs justification . . . that the dramatic character of what she did and suffered, consists" (pp. 276–77), terms Shelley "the most restless casuist of them all."[48] Now that

[48]Smith, p. 85.

40

Pieracci has come to light, Shelley must take rank below him as a casuist. If, as seems likely, Shelley had the example of Pieracci before him, he evinces a restraint that is truly remarkable in altering the account in Beatrice's justification no more than he has. Nothing in Shelley matches Pieracci's casuistry in presenting the essential legendary account of the murder yet masking in ambiguity her role in it, as well as that of Olimpio and Marzio. We know that Cenci died violently and in what manner, but who did it? Almost everybody—Marzio, Olimpio, Cammillo, Ippolito, and Beatrice—competes for the title of self-sacrificing hero(ine), and Beatrice wins handily. In those prefatory remarks of his, Shelley may well have had Pieracci in mind.

A recapitulation of the evidence for the *Beatrice Cenci* as a source is in order here. Shelley has ten close parallels to Pieracci not to be found in Es: the character name of Cammillo/Camillo; the function of Cammillo/Camillo; the Sovereign/Pope's refusal to weigh Cenci's crimes against his murder; Beatrice's denial of acquaintance with the murderer(s); a crowd hostile to Beatrice; Beatrice's sense of the continuing evil power of Cenci after his death; the presence of retributive, telltale objects in the environment; a complex figure combining sun, blackness, sky, and blood; in combination with this figure, a figure in which Beatrice appears to be polluting or polluted; and a mad scene of Beatrice in both plays in which appears a nexus of the last two parallel figures.

In addition to these ten close parallels between Pieracci and Shelley there are a number of facts and inclinations, not in Es, that both playwrights share. Since there is some divergence and Shelley makes his own his source materials, we cannot be certain that Pieracci is or is not his source in these materials: both reduce the traditional violence and gore and Cenci's sexual exploits, though Shelley adds incestuous rape, and each does so in different ways; both try, as far as possible, to exculpate Beatrice in the murder of Cenci but in opposite ways; both have Beatrice's petition to the Pope withheld from him but by different agencies; Beatrice in both plays doubts Providence at different places and for individual reasons; both playwrights have the incriminating look of fear at different places and for different purposes; both have much imagery for the external projection of inner states, Pieracci for aftereffect, Shelley in anticipation; both have hallucinatory response from physical surroundings but for different characters; both have characters anatomizing their inner states but with different content; and both have their heroines alive at the curtain but facing different deaths. Some of these nine similarities seem more persuasively Pieraccian than others.

It was indicated at the outset that what Shelley did or did not use of Pieracci would yield insights into his creative process. At various points in the study, an effort has been made to show some of these insights. In conclusion, it would be well to bring these together and evaluate them. Adhering to the traditional neoclassical unities of time and place, and a comparatively simple concentration of dramatic tension, Pieracci opens his play after the murder of Francesco Cenci, and his one area of conflict is between Beatrice and the court of justice. Staying closer to the legendary account of Es and desiring as many areas of tension as possible, Shelley begins his play before the murder, includes the murder, and ends just before the executions. He has two main areas of conflict in succession: 1) between Beatrice and Cenci, and 2) between Beatrice and the forces of law. Like Pieracci he compresses the time scope, but to some weeks instead of one day, enough to increase the tempo of the legend and heighten the sense of inevitability of action and outcome. To increase the areas of tension he adds to Pieracci's one, successful attempt at murder the one given earlier in Es. For the same reason he adds from Es three more co-conspirators—Giacomo, Lucretia, and the priest Orsino —to those Pieracci has involved in the murder—Beatrice, and the two retainers, Olimpio and Marzio. Orsino corresponds to Guerra, a co-conspirator in the legendary account—Guerra, whom Pieracci has reduced to a close confidant of Beatrice, with a suggestion of love interest. For additional dramatice tension Shelley devised various false clues not found elsewhere: approaching footsteps turn out not to be those of the dreaded Cenci but of a friendly person. Immediately after the murder a horn announces not "some tedious guest" as expected but the deadly papal Legate Savella. Other sources of tension, many of them from Pieracci, will be summarized below.

To create a play acceptable to the public both Pieracci and Shelley reduce the raw violence of the legendary account, and both attempt in so far as possible to exculpate Beatrice. These two motives go hand in hand. Pieracci's Cenci dies of precisely three stab wounds, a fact which seems to eliminate Beatrice's participation. Shelley's dies bloodlessly, by strangulation. Both playwrights omit Cenci's attempt, which Shelley for one found in Es, at persuasive incest with Beatrice as dramatically unacceptable. Pieracci makes so ambiguous Beatrice's connection with the murder that she may have had no part in it at all. This he does by contradictions in the account of Olimpio and Marzio, her denying acquaintance with the presumed murderers, having the provocation to murder falling preponderantly on the two retainers, and putting part of the blame on Aldobrando, friend of Cenci, who withheld Beatrice's petition before the murder. Shelley, to the same end but keeping closer to the account in Es, pursues an opposite strategy. He makes Beatrice clearly guilty but less so than in Es by two endeavors: 1) a distribution of the guilt, and 2) increasing her provocation to murder. He has the murder suggestion arising in five minds simultaneously and independently instead of principally Beatrice's, and after many earlier abuses Cenci rapes his daughter. Not only does Beatrice surrender her role as ringleader to the priest Orsino, but it is he who is responsible for the treacherous deed Pieracci lays to Aldobrando of withholding Beatrice's petition before the murder. Thus Beatrice's guilt diminishes as her provocation increases. Her denying acquaintance with Olimpio and Marzio, which Pieracci originated to becloud Beatrice's guilt, Shelley uses to offer Beatrice a desperate possibility of escape and to demonstrate her valor in the face of hostile destiny.

Shelley has other means too of reducing the raw violence of the legendary account. With an eye to the audience he reduces Cenci's previous crimes from sodomy to the more stageworthy murder and reserves his assault on theatrical convention for incestuous rape, masking it in "delicacy." Aesthetically, he tells us, writing of his play in general, he increases the ideal and diminishes the horror to let pleasure mitigate the pain for the audience of contemplating moral depravity.

Perhaps the most striking borrowing of Shelley from Pieracci is the character of Camillo (Cammillo in Pieracci). Besides being a confidant of Beatrice in a familiar neoclassical role, he is also for Pieracci a would-be intercessor for her with the Sovereign and her would-be rescuer from painful associations. Shelley keeps him in his role as ineffectual pleader, but makes him a cardinal to fit him for a much enlarged function in his play than in Pieracci's. In somewhat more than the first half of the play, Camillo acts as liaison between Cenci and the Pope. In the second part he intercedes for Beatrice with the Pope. His failure to rescue Beatrice heightens the tension of the last scene. Perhaps seeing this potential moved Shelley to borrow him from Pieracci.

Pieracci offers Shelley a great many suspense-building elements, but he operates at disadvantages Shelley has avoided. Since Pieracci's Beatrice is present and talking about herself throughout the play, he seems to set Shelley an example in character "self-anatomy," but since her role, in the murder, if any, is never clear, all her self-revelations have to be on side issues, in avoidance of the main questions: did she have a hand in killing Cenci? if so, in what manner? Consequently her "self-anatomy" does not build much tension. She may be revealed as innocent and cleared—exactly the line the judge Marsilio does take. Shelley reveals Beatrice's guilty role from the beginning, and she can go on with a complete "self-anatomy" that intensifies our interest in her character and fate as the main questions unroll: will she kill Cenci? will she escape punishment?

Furthermore, since Cenci is already dead when Pieracci's play opens, and Pieracci is building to only one climax, at the end, he scatters his tension-creating elements throughout. Since Shelley builds to two climaxes, the murder of Cenci and the leading to the scaffold, he concentrates the major power of these elements at the more important of these two climaxes, in the last two scenes of the play. Pieracci also puts the strongest of his elements, the mad scene, at the best place for him, at the end. But with several elements from Pieracci at his disposal, Shelley can afford to move his great mad scene back to the beginning of the third act, just after the incestuous rape of Beatrice, where its hallucinatory revelation of Beatrice's inner state prepares for acceptance of Cenci's murder.

Other tension-building elements contributed from various

parts of Pieracci's play Shelley concentrates in the penultimate and last scene to make understandable Beatrice's fall into despair, in spite of her strength, before her rise to a noble acceptance of her fate; such is frequently a part of tragic structure. Before her strange confession Beatrice anticipates an unsympathetic crowd at her execution. Word comes by Camillo that the implacable Pope has refused to balance off her murder of Cenci with his crimes against the family, especially the rape of Beatrice; the execution must proceed. An almost hallucinatory obsession, supplied by Pieracci, emerges in Beatrice in the last scene that the evil power of her father persists even after his death, adding to her sense of inescapable doom. As the end approaches Beatrice begins to doubt the goodness of providence toward her as does Pieracci's Beatrice at the very end. At that point, of course, Shelley's Beatrice finds her own inner strength.

Equally true for *The Cenci* is what Shelley says of his dramatic imagery in the Preface of *Prometheus Unbound*, that it may be "drawn from the operations of the human mind, or from those external actions by which they are expressed." In the Preface to *The Cenci* he says his dramatic images are "employed in the illustration of strong feeling." Many of the most passionate images of Shelley that he has borrowed from Pieracci put mental states in physical terms. Thinking of her connection with her father's murder, whatever that is, Pieracci's Beatrice says she is like a source of pollution to those about her. From an object of self-abhorrence, a type of polluting cause, she becomes in Shelley's mad scene a type of polluted victim. This imagerial coup d'état of Shelley, like many of his other dramatic elements, is made possible by his keeping Cenci alive for the first three acts to victimize his daughter. Another example would be helpful. In their mad scenes both Beatrices — one poisoned, the other raped — project their disorientation into complex, hallucinatory, imagery of sun, blackness, sky, and blood. This projection into externals intensifies what has happened to them. Shelley has not much altered his imagery or its application. Projection may take another form. Both playwrights have guilty, or soon-to-be-guilty, souls aware of telltale objects in their environment. What is not much developed in Pieracci becomes hallucinatory in Shelley's

45

Cenci, enhancing dramatic tension. If we may assume as existing an example of connection between the two plays that has been conservatively kept in the doubtful group: for one of the most interesting revelations of Shelley's reshaping hand at work, let us examine what he quite likely has done with the fear of Pieracci's Beatrice that her look of fear may incriminate her. He intensifies Pieracci's image by implanting the basilisk in it and puts it in Beatrice's mouth to minimize the incriminating effect of Lucretia's fainting during the arrest scene when they hear they must go to Rome for trial. This underlines Beatrice's strength and presence of mind.

One last point: both playwrights have Beatrice near death but alive at the curtain. Since no continuing action is contemplated in either play after her death, this is the point of highest interest and poignancy in the plays, where the audience experiences catharsis and the heroine rises to acceptance of her fate. Pieracci's heroine is to meet death by suicide, at a time when she is under no external compulsion to die. Such a death as hers makes the victim an example of noble self-sacrifice but never seems so tragic as an involuntary death, societally imposed, in which the victim must meet death with whatever inner resources he can summon, small man crushed but fighting to the last against forces greater than himself. Shelley stays close to the legend, and his heroine dies in this fashion.

In the next section, Pieracci's Italian play and the English translation, in reverse order.

Appendix A

It is not part of this study to determine what Pieracci read for *his* play, only what Pieracci supplied Shelley that Shelley could not get from his Italian manuscript, but some remarks about the relationship of both plays to the Italian accounts of the Cenci legend that both drew upon would be of interest. In shaping the Cenci story to the Alfierian dramatic form and his own desires, Pieracci has departed so far from the known accounts, which, for all Professor Steffan's careful differentiation, are relatively homogeneous, that any one of several could have supplied nearly all of Pieracci's materials. It would be difficult if not impossible to fix upon any particular one as his source. Versions C, D, or F could supply Pieracci with the detail that Beatrice's petition to the Pope was not available to its designated recipient, and D alone could supply him with the moralizing of Beatrice's last speech in which she calls upon children and parents to exercise the greatest possible forbearance toward each other.[1] Against this positive evidence favoring D is some negative evidence—the argument from silence, for what it is worth—favoring Shelley's

---

[1]Steffan, pp. 614–15.

Es. Like Pieracci, Es alone does not have the Pope/Sovereign balancing off the crimes of the father against those of the children, though for a time favorably impressed by a similar weighing by the advocate Farinacci; does not have so much vulgarity as the others; and omits most of the pietistic element of the other versions.[2] Since there must, of course, be other versions not known to Steffan, it is practically impossible to determine with any certainty what version or versions Pieracci may have read. As for Shelley, Es, which he follows with considerable fidelity, remains his primary source, and Pieracci becomes his secondary source.

---

[2]Steffan, pp. 616–17.

Appendix B

Each playwright in his own way has a curious practice of delving into his background reading for names and, in a few instances, situations, and adopting them to a new role. Pieracci's Ippolito Guerra, close friend of Beatrice, owes his surname to the Italian legend, but his given name, Ippolito, is the given name of Ippolito Aldobrandini, Pope Clement VIII, who made the final decision in the Cenci case. There are other examples. Aldobrando, the friend of Count Cenci who withholds Beatrice's petition in Pieracci, is an obvious nomenclatural offspring of "Aldobrandini," the singular form shortened by one syllable.

When Pieracci invented the name of Cammillo Farnese, the influential close friend of Beatrice, he was probably inspired for the given name by a source similar to Ippolito's. At the death of Clement VIII in 1605, he was succeeded by Leo XI, whose pontificate of less than one month was succeeded by that of Camillo Borghese, Paul V. A Farnese's influence with the "Sovereign" might come naturally; Clement VIII rose to power through the favor of Cardinal Alessandro Farnese, and Ranuccio Farnese (1569–1622), Duke of Parma, married Margherita Aldobrandina. There is no Camillo, or Cammillo, Farnese of the time. Pieracci has been careful to play down any clear association of the church with the Cenci case, but for some reason he weaves into the fabric three church-connected names of the time not readily so identifiable. He attaches two names to people sympathetic to Beatrice, one to an unsympathic person.

Ulysse Moracci, the judge of Es and other accounts[3] who was replaced by the Pope on suspicion that he was too much under the influence of Beatrice's beauty, switches his role to the sympathetic side in Pieracci, who has Fausto suggesting that "Ulisse" be allowed to undertake Beatrice's defense (II, ix, p. 50). Clement VIII may not appear by name in *Beatrice Cenci*, but Cammillo reports the "holy old man" who is the "Sovereign" indulging one of Clement's recorded weaknesses, a readiness to tears:[4] he weeps over Beatrice's just-discovered petition (III, iv, p. 72).

Shelley also has acquired knowledge of the Cenci background, and though he stays closer to his original than Pieracci, he too applies creativity to the names and roles. When Camillo reminds Cenci that he has saved Cenci's life three times, and Cenci replies, "For which Aldobrandino owes you now/ My fief beyond the Pincian" (I, i, 56–58), we hark back to Camillo's opening lines and discover that the Aldobrandino in question is the Pope: "That matter of the murder is hushed up/ If you consent to yield his Holiness/ Your fief that lies beyond the Pincian gate." The only significant way in which this departs from history and the legend is in changing sodomy to murder; and when Shelley makes Camillo a cardinal and influencial nephew of the Pope, he adopts the given name in Pieracci but retains the historical role. Two of Clement VIII's nephews were cardinals, and one of them, Cardinal Pietro Aldobrandini, especially enjoyed his favor and stood at his right hand.[5] A third nephew, Giovan Francesco Aldobrandini, general of the papal armies, is no doubt the nephew of Cenci's words: "Ay, I once heard the nephew of the Pope/ Had sent his architect to view the ground,/ Meaning to build a villa on my vines/ The next time I compounded with his uncle" (I, i,

[3]Steffan, pp. 615: C, D, Es have "Ulysse Moraci"; F has "Ulysses Moscatti."
[4]Ricci, II, 141–42.
[5]Ricci, I, 242–43.

16–19). Shelley has preserved the historical sequence by allowing the Count to look into the future. After the murder, executions, and papal confiscation of the Cenci property, Giovan Francesco was allowed to purchase the Cenci estate of Torrenova without having to prove himself the highest bidder, as had been stipulated earlier.[6]

For two names Shelley resorted to quite a bit of adapting. Probably becasue he was making considerable changes in the role, especially feeling Pieracci's utterly harmless Ippolito Guerra as an insupportable contrast, he needed to change the name of Guerra. For what he had in mind he had to return to the Guerra of Es and then recreate him in a more evil form, but Pieracci had spoiled the name for his purposes. It is difficult to determine which of the Orsini Shelley had in mind for "Orsino,"[7] but this most powerful of the princely Roman families had long been head of the Guelph, or papal, faction in its conflict with the Ghibellines. Influential in church policy, they numbered among them four cardinals and a pope. The church could draw upon them for soldiers, statesmen, and prelates. At the time of the Cenci case and later an Orsini was regularly prince assistant to the pope. At least a few members of the family resemble Shelley's Orsino. In the early 1580's Paolo Giordano Orsini—who, it is supposed, had already had his wife murdered—now it seems procured the murder of Francesco Peretti, whose wife he desired. As soon as circumstances permitted, he married the widow, Vittoria Accoramboni, whose brother Marcello had murdered Peretti. Soon afterward he died, poisoned, it is said, at the instigation of one of his first wife's relatives. In the same year, 1585, Vittoria and her brother Flamineo were stabbed to death at the behest of Lodovico Orsini, who believed she had degraded the family. One of Shelley's favorite authors, John Webster, has a well-known play on the subject, *The White Devil, or Vittoria Corombona* (pub. 1612).

The readiest at hand of Shelley's adapted names, and the

---

[6]Ricci, II, 223–24.

[7]Changing the ending of an Italian name in number or gender has not been considered good practice, but it is sometimes done. Shelley has already changed Aldobrandini to Aldobrandino in I, i, 57.

one farthest separated from its source, is that of Savella, the papal legate who arrests the Cenci. One of their places of imprisonment in the manuscript is Corte Savella (Es, pp. 406, 407, 408, 413), so named for the much-propertied Savelli family of Rome who had jurisdiction over this tribunal.

Part II

Beatrice Cenci

DRAMATIS PERSONAE

Beatrice
Cammillo
Ippolito
Marsilio
Fausto
Marzio
Olimpio
Soldiers

Male Servants
Female Servants   of Beatrice

The scene is in Rome in the house of Beatrice.

53

ACT I

Scene i

CAMMILLO, BEATRICE

CAMMILLO.

Express your feelings freely, Beatrice, to one whose heart cherishes true friendship for you. Silence would be only an inappropriate or unusual consideration. Rome, I see clearly, has become a place of horrible mourning. You cannot have an hour of peace where the terrible fate of your unhappy father resounds on everybody's lips. Now banish that downcast expression, and resolve to leave this country. I offer myself as your protective escort. My age still virile by nature but about to succumb to the weight of an already completed sixtieth year and the not ignoble acclaim of my reputation free you from the judgment of the world. Sad evils often are overcome by change of place, by the observing of kingdoms and provinces, new customs and habits. I am telling you what I myself know by experience. Experience to which one adds his own salutary advice, makes me speak up for your good only.

BEATRICE.

Your indomitable Farnese stock shines ever and ever more pure in your deeds, in your liberal ways. Your understanding friendship will always be engraved in the depth of my heart, O Cammillo. I ought to accept your kind invitation, ought to flee from this fateful place, and never return again. . . . O miserable me! . . . Ah, where can I go that I do not always draw my cruel sorrow with me!

CAMMILLO.

Sorrow has its limits. Are we perchance born to live in tears? Where is that soul from whom death has not dared to snatch some beloved object! Time conquers not only unhappy memories but the happy ones as well. I know that your father's end was atrocious, also not in the regular course of

54

nature and deserves more filial weeping; yet your coming out of your incessant sorrow would not only be a virtue but a duty required by the obligation to live.

BEATRICE.

I understand well enought my natural duty. I would like to conquer my anguish, to dry up the spring of sad fantasies, to breathe pleasant air, finally to cease weeping. But, sir, I cannot: my fierce sorrow is beyond control.

CAMMILLO.

Can the cause of your sorrow be the sad memory your father left in Rome? How can one excuse the pride with which he sometimes decked out his deeds, and his aggressive, ferocious temperment? You were the too loving daughter of a licentious father: it must be said now. Who led him on to the precipitous rock? Does a rational mind ever run toward a precipice? Beatrice, I want to take you away from these cheerless walls. Second my vows; don't be obstinate. I am yearning to give you back a father. Heaven itself by granting nobility to your face, dignity and superior thought, condemns your useless sadness.

BEATRICE.

I am condemned in the wrath of heaven.

CAMMILLO.

But how! What evil can exist without remedy? Tell me, could the pangs of love be tormenting you? . . . Even if it were so . . . Love will not be guilty. . . . Reveal your soul to me; no one can hear us: speak, is your lover a man of low estate? I cannot believe him a wicked soul. Be at ease: I have means to give him status. Tell me his name.

BEATRICE.

Ah my sweet friend! . . . but one who comes running! . . .

CAMMILLO.

Ipplitio seems to me . . . but tell . . . .

BEATRICE.

Ah love does not torture me, O Cammillo! Alas, there are some born to misfortune. There are some who must never be happy. . . . What's happening?

Scene ii.

IPPOLITO, BEATRICE, CAMMILLO.

IPPOLITO.

> I'm bringing incredible news. . . . Oh times! The sacred vaults where the shades have refuge are no longer safe. There are some who dare with sacrilegious hand to drag your father's body from its quiet tomb. . . .

BEATRICE.

> Oh, woe is me! What are you telling? . . . The tremor of death shakes my whole body.

CAMMILLO.

> What reason is given for this action?

IPPOLITO.

> Fierce suspicions made their way into the Sovereign's mind. He doesn't believe that Francesco, infuriated, desperate, completely irrational, could have hurled himself from the balcony of his house on to the deep rock. On the contrary, fearing that it was most treacherously done by someone who took his life in a rage, he now is having the body examined.

BEATRICE.

> Does he who reigns also rule over the dead?

CAMILLO.

> Do you know the results of the order?

IPPOLITO.

> As soon as the body was out of the tomb I was anxious to run to Beatrice.

BEATRICE.

> And the living breezes did not disdainfully flee from the cold body? Didn't guilty night cover at once the profaned sacred refuge? Didn't heaven thunder on the wicked hands set upon the deed? . . . And should I live on? And I should live happy, O Cammillo!

CAMMILLO.

> The act is horrible: but a ruler can never be too vigilant, Beatrice. Who knows that the suspicion may not be just? Who knows that chance may not have brought forth evi-

56

dence on Francesco's fate? It is true that he was arrogant, intractable, proud; harmful to others, an evil of nature, and dangerous to himself . . . . But who can tell the world why he died? Who knows, some fierce, capable enemy of his may have dared to thrust his foot deeply into his home? And what valor does it take to kill a man in sleep or caught unaware? Then the highest cunning instructs one to cover up the crime. The rock was there for this purpose.

BEATRICE.
What story are you telling? Where were we? . . . But, oh savagery of things! . . . Enough, everything happens to make me the most unhappy object in nature . . . . I want to be left alone a moment with my sad thoughts. You have the most perfect soul, O Cammillo. I want to leave you only for a little. Ippolito, also go the same way as your friend and then return . . . . But no . . . how daring I am! You are too much the followers of irreproachable virtue. Miserable woman as I am, I am not worthy of binding you to me . . . . Oh God! And is it possible that I drive virtue away? . . . I see it well! No sorrow exists that can kill.

IPPOLITO.
Such news had to fill your heart with a daughter's repugnance. The steps of justice, however, are unfettered, and from now on you must endure the despotic function . . . . I hear people drawing near . . . .

CAMMILLO.
Soldiers in arms! . . .

Scene iii

Fausto, *with a following of Soldiers*, Beatrice, Cammillo, Ippolito

BEATRICE.
What are you coming for?
FAUSTO.
Are you Beatrice?

BEATRICE.

I am.

FAUSTO.

Quickly assemble all the men servants and maidservants of your house. You will await the order to leave here . . . . Soldiers, guard all the entrances.

BEATRICE.

Do you have the Sovereign order?

FAUSTO.

Not open to question. You may see it if you wish.

BEATRICE.

No more. Lorenzo! Assemble immediately the servants of the house, my people; bring them here. *(Lorenzo goes out at this moment.)*

IPPOLITO.

What a procedure!

CAMMILLO.

Mortal anguish, which plumbs the depths of Beatrice's heart, this much is certain. I don't understand such severity. Adverse fortune puts friends to the test. Listen: I make myself responsible for all . . . .

FAUSTO.

This is a high command; I cannot give in under any condition.

CAMMILLO.

At least don't conceal the reason for this.

BEATRICE.

And what if the cause of this should be a secret wickedness, who will make amends to one's reputation?

FAUSTO.

Revealed innocence makes amends for everything.

BEATRICE.

And who can suppress the fear of the soul?

FAUSTO.

Where is there fear without crime?

BEATRICE.

There are souls whose innocence cannot keep fear, often fatal, from entering.

FAUSTO.

The Magistrate's habitual practice is never fallible in assuring
him of the truth.

BEATRICE.

Does guilt lie here?

FAUSTO.

I just obey the order.

BEATRICE.

Well then, you are at liberty to do as you please; there are my
servants.

(The men and women in Beatrice's service enter.)

FAUSTO.

Select one among them from each sex: suit yourself about the
choice.

BEATRICE.

And the others?

FAUSTO.

They will be safe; don't fear.

BEATRICE.

First I want to know each one's fate.

FAUSTO.

I can't reassure you.

BEATRICE.

Well then, Teresa, you stay with me, and Lorenzo. Tell me,
will I have the authority to provide for whoever goes.

FAUSTO.

It's up to you.

BEATRICE.

Lorenzo, take this . . . . *(She gives him a key.)* Fortune denied
me peace, but not money: from this you may give them
generously whatever amount you want. You know where
they are taken: you will tell me about it later.

FAUSTO.

You there! Accompany these people; and you . . . .

CAMMILLO.

Let us speak! Rome knows me, the Sovereign knows me well.

No thought of any misdeed enters my mind; nor do I frequent a house sympathetic to crime. Now mark: I believe I'm worthy of understanding, of knowing what the cause may be of this most solemn array. I wish to ward off fear from, and restore the honor of, so many people. I have great wealth and power. I don't oppose the law nor do I change it. I would want only to avoid so much public talk.

FAUSTO.

Did you hear? At a better time you will reveal your noble heart.

End of the First Act.

ACT II

Scene i

IPPOLITO, BEATRICE

IPPOLITO.

I don't know myself any more. Why are we hemmed in by people lost to compassion, full of harshness. Beatrice, oh God! What may we fear? Did they perhaps discover from your father's cold body evidence from which derive such severe measures against us? I have no peace of mind. In addition I heard a while ago that they arrested outside of Rome both of your servants who had disappeared, Marzio and Olimpio.

BEATRICE.

They arrested Olimpio and Marzio?

IPPOLITO.

Those two people gone from you after the lamentable accident happened, aroused suspicion, as you know, and justice did not slacken the pursuit of them for one day. When they were finally caught, who knows what lying confession for their flight they might not have fabricated. Then with great expedition here we have the body examined, immediately we have Francesco's dry body pulled out of the tomb. Then from thinking about the fierce deed which had taken place at your house, here comes severity for all, here we are all involved in suspicion . . . . But what happened, Beatrice? You were sadder before knowing this news. I admire the stoutness of your heart. Bitter circumstances distinguish spirits, and constancy overcomes the enmity of adverse fate.

BEATRICE.

But I am not happy. Anguish pours into my heart in torrents, and when they reach my eyes my tears turn to stone . . . . Cammillo, tell me, where is he? Why don't I see him at my side?

IPPOLITO.

He writes in complete devotion; he will come shortly . . . . Oh sad fate of our souls. When most sweet marriage could have united those that virtue and nature ever had vied to produce . . . .

BEATRICE.

Be silent: don't make that repressed fatal anguish of mine burst forth in weeping, or in spasms of death. Love, that I have seen grow ever more beautiful and dearer with each increasing year, has disappeared from my eyes. Wherever I may go, the breezes for me become poison. Not for one hour have I peace. On my very featherbed, widowed always of tranquil sleep, I bear only anguish . . . . Ah no! Let us talk no more of anguish. Don't irritate a burdened heart with your words . . . . Now is the time to dare. We must think of protecting my honor from the cruel assaults of enemy destiny . . . . Hello! Who is coming? Call Cammillo immediately.

Scene ii

MARSILIO, BEATRICE.

MARSILIO.

You must be Beatrice.

61

BEATRICE.

You named me.

MARSILIO.

Now, get used to facing the stern presence of an uncorrupted judge. No one need have fear before committing a crime. The error of man, first-born and father of guilty passion, degraded man . . . . But enough of rationalizing! So endowed as you are with heavenly beauty, can you have knowledge of crimes? Trouble under cruel necessity grants as much. Answer me without fear. Where are your people?

BEATRICE.

The order sent them away. Only two of my people remain.

MARSILIO.

All right. Teresa is one, the other Lorenzo. *(Silently looking at a sheet he has with him.)* There are two more . . . .

BEATRICE.

Friends . . . .

MARSILIO.

You are right: *(Continuing to read as above.)* Cammillo Farnese and Ippolito Guerra. You will retire into the next room, and have Cammillo come here.

Scene iii

CAMMILLO, MARSILIO.

CAMMILLO.

What is wanted of me?

MARSILIO.

Sir, you are a friend of such great integrity that I cannot find it in me to imagine in you the least shadow of guilt.

CAMMILLO.

Speak out: do your job without other considerations.

MARSILIO.

It suits me. The steadfast law removes all these. Tell me: have you known Beatrice for long?

CAMMILLO.

She grew up in my arms.

62

MARSILIO.

A firm friendship alone has always motivated your seeing her?

CAMMILLO.

Never any other desire.

MARSILIO.

You are incapable of lying, Sir. Take now the liberty your own house affords you.

CAMMILLO.

Listen . . . .

MARSILIO.

Pardon, Sir: It is time for obedience, not words. This is a serious case. Soldiers, escort him.

CAMMILLO.

I'm asking a favor. Keep your escort. I'll go to my house with Ippolito.

MARSILIO.

I must hear him.

CAMMILLO.

You can do that later. Let my sacred word be his guaranty.

MARSILIO.

Hey, soldiers! Allow free passage to Ippolito, to Cammillo.

Scene iv

IPPOLITO, CAMMILLO, MARSILIO.

CAMMILLO.

Friend, join me . . . .

IPPOLITO.

And we will not even say goodbye to Beatrice! . . . What an unheard-of kind of torture!

MARSILIO.

No one is to enter here any longer who has not been called, to take away the servants who have been assigned.

CAMMILLO.

Let's go. Hope does not abandon my footsteps. I have already written to the Prince of Rome asking to speak with him: no day passes that I don't see and hear him. I will obtain the favor I'm sure: he himself will tell me what fate has put the young lady in jeopardy.

IPPOLITO.

May your pure friendship, Sir, protect her honor.

Scene v

MARSILIO.

Since those people have gone, I am going to see the accused young girl again. Bring Beatrice again before me. I still cannot imagine her tainted by such a wicked crime; nevertheless there is a great suspicion that she is guilty .... Before the investigation I will try to see if in a measure I can discover her heart. Young as she is she cannot prove as crafty as a man red with guilt would be in concealing himself: and if she should be really innocent, I want to console her and remove her every fear. But if she should have boldly trespassed over the limit of any law, it is requisite then to give free rein to an unexampled severity .... There she is.

Scene vi

BEATRICE, MARSILIO

MARSILIO.

I am very much afraid, young woman, that I am bothering you. However, dedicated to the law and the Tribunal, where I bear a firm exterior and a trembling heart, I must be in spite of myself bothersome. Doesn't my presence inspire in your heart the motions of fear?

BEATRICE.

What! Are you clothed in cruelty?

MARSILIO.

I am clothed according to the cases. A heart not guilty always finds me gentle. Differently the guilty. I desire to hear from you what consideration a criminal deserves.

BEATRICE.

That same consideration that the one who condemns him has in his heart.

MARSILIO.

A wise soul so answers. He who has mirth in his countenance does not have war in his heart. Your happy appearance reassures me. Can there be any harm for the honest person? Go on. You are the target of adverse inconceivable, enemy cruelty. Overcome it: disperse it, make the slanderers vanish. At the harmonious sound of public voices honored echo will answer from the seven hills. You will hear hymns of praise, and the festive daughters of Rome in white dresses will all come running, O Beatrice, to rejoice with you.

BEATRICE.

(Bursts into the most unrestrained weeping.)

MARSILIO.

What! You are weeping! . . .

BEATRICE.

Oh God! What am I doing before such a terrible judge? . . . Sir, no, don't believe, no, don't believe that my weeping is born of deeds to be sorry for.

MARSILIO.

Calm down and hide it. Immense tenderness, desire of a good reputation move your tears. You certainly are not guilty . . . but uproar rises from the streets of Rome. I listen to the name that they pronounce, yours.

Scene vii

FAUSTO, BEATRICE, MARSILIO.

MARSILIO.

Fausto, tell the motives for the sudden popular uproar.

65

FAUSTO.

The bold Roman people demand to see Beatrice. The door defended by soldiers makes your residence here secure.

MARSILIO.

Watch: in a few moments Marzio and Olimpio will enter. Hold them for me.

FAUSTO.

She sighs; oh late repentance!

MARSILIO.

And there aren't any other tears? . . . New clamors arise. Go look, Fausto, and return.

Scene viii.

MARSILIO, BEATRICE

MARSILIO.

You must have courage, young lady; you will hear that they consider you guilty of a deed, such a deed as breaks every bond of nature. I want to tell you this ahead of time, although this is contrary to custom, so that you may fortify your soul. Your heart shifts about too much from instant to instant. I would have you always show the same expression.

BEATRICE.

I shudder at the devices of guilt, and he must shudder whose soul is hostile to guilt.

Scene ix.

FAUSTO, BEATRICE, MARSILIO.

FAUSTO.

Here are, Sir, Cristiano and Ulisse, famous masterminds, highest ornaments of the Forum, and unfailing hopes of him who appears smeared with a serious accusation. They offer themselves of their own accord for the suspected lady's great defense.

BEATRICE.

    (With great force of spirit.)

I am not guilty; only a traitor can make me suspect; I fear nothing; therefore with head held high I have no need of the lofty spirits who may support those who are wicked. I will have the ability to defend myself. I myself will make a shield for me.

FAUSTO.

See what courage all of a sudden!

MARSILIO.

Well then, within an hour. . . .

BEATRICE.

You will see me.

MARSILIO.

I await you.

End of the Second Act.

ACT III

Scene i

FAUSTO, *SERGEANT.*

FAUSTO.

Severity has increased. Don't let anyone pass before I know it, except someone who should have the Sovereign order.

Scene ii

IPPOLITO *disguised,* FAUSTO

FAUSTO.

Who are you?

IPPOLITO.

Lorenzo, servant of Beatrice.

FAUSTO.

You are not forbidden entrance.

IPPOLITO.

Love and a fervent desire to be of service to the lady have protected my difficult undertaking.

FAUSTO.

Listen to me . . . .

IPPOLITO.

Oh heaven! Now he finds me out. . . . What do you want of me?

FAUSTO.

You are going to her!

IPPOLITO.

Exactly.

FAUSTO.

You will tell her that in a few moments the fateful hour ends.

Scene iii

BEATRICE, IPPOLITO

BEATRICE.

Lorenzo!

IPPOLITO.

Let us maintain the deception, Beatrice. . . .

BEATRICE.

Oh the voice! Lorenzo! . . . Oh God! You in this attire?

IPPOLITO.

Heaven favored my plan. I am running to you as a bearer of bad news. Your honor, your very life, your property seem in great peril. The clamor that you are guilty arises throughout Rome. There is no escape for you: after the harshest trial you will hear pronounced the cruel sentence of death. Such ferocious events and such fearful possibilities so combine that there is no power to defend you. The Sovereign of Rome is seething. He wants you to serve as a baleful example to posterity. I am not considering your anguish: I only desire to reveal to you the truth. Save your life: you have little time, you will come with me. The exit that leads the way to the dungeon, traversing the garden in a vast circle, is still open. Do not delay; be resolved . . . Beatrice . . . . Oh heaven! Thus you await infamy!

BEATRICE.

True friend, Ippolito, truly noble spirit! I praise highly your deeds, not your counsel, which if I follow it will bring me no less infamy than I will have in remaining. Who flees? The cowardly, or the soul who is lost to hope, who has guilt in his heart, certainly not he who loves honor, and life, and all that is sweet in the universe. The test is fierce. I know the whole dimension of my misfortune. I would give up money, the immense property that I possess, and this my youth, and the gifts of nature, taking on even a misshapen old age, and the status of a servant, to escape intact from deadly judgment. Hope still, that good that never abandons whoever breathes; still a sure courage, that I feel within me, not always fragile face to face with virtue, will sustain me, will give me valor. Then all of us corrupted by time, which consumes us, we will lie in little dust. Fate guides our feet to the tomb. We live for the tomb; we live with error that ages us, in the midst of evil that endures, and of good that is a dream.

IPPOLITO.

Beatrice, you spoke truly; but sometimes trust deceives us. A bold step never is the one that saves. Times removes every memory; then we lose even the idea, the purpose of what has been.

BEATRICE.

And what is the purpose of life without honor? . . .

IPPOLITO.

Hush: I want to save both for you. Give up: walk rapidly; every moment gold cannot buy.

BEATRICE.

Who is coming?

IPPOLITO.

Oh escape this savage moment! . . .

BEATRICE.

And you don't see it? Your disguise can increase the damage. Save my honor, my honor which is put in terrible danger. . . . Ah go! The noise is getting nearer.

IPPOLITO.

I don't want to leave you in such grave danger. . . .

BEATRICE.

Then is this your love for me? . . . Hide: with me truth itself is suspect.

IPPOLITO.

I'm going, if you want that; but really not far: I want to hear the outcome of the fateful examination.

Scene iv

CAMMILLO, BEATRICE

CAMMILLO.

The Prince allows me to see you.

BEATRICE.

Oh God! Cammillo! . . . oh sight! oh lovable sight! You are great indeed if you remember a lady so enveloped in horror.

CAMMILLO.

Beatrice!

BEATRICE.

Wretched me! . . . What happened? I read in your face that you are disturbed.

CAMMILLO.

Listen: the rumor about you that runs through the streets of Rome gives me fierce torment. I still can't believe it true. Beatrice! I used to see in you all the feelings of tenderness; I used to watch you grow up, develop, give a beautiful demonstration of filial love, and all the rays of virtue shine about you.

BEATRICE.

Ah do you want to see me dead of sorrow? . . . I feel consumed within myself. . . . A superior force invades me. Before my eyes I see everything change . . . Cammillo! it is true; I have the look of a guilty person. Tyrannous furies, wickedness, of which there is no equal, conspire to my damage. The duty of an honorable soul is to forget me. I deserve to be abandoned by all, now that I have become an object of loathing. . . . Where am I? Why do I remain alive! The loss of life would be sweet to my heart; but to lose honor, reputation, your friendship, Cammillo, would weave about my heart such a dark calamity that I would see myself insane, resolved to look for a weapon and, desperate, to take my life even though innocent.

CAMMILLO.

My heart does not change, be sure: shortly we will find out. Meanwhile hear the protestations of friendship. If I cannot overcome the harsh measures of the implacable judge, I can alleviate them in part: with liberal means I can open a way for me, where one could have least expected it.

BEATRICE.

And so you believe me guilty?

CAMMILLO.

I am beside myself! The Sovereign just now was reckoning up your deeds for me. . . .

BEATRICE.

Just now! . . . Sir, don't speak to me of him. . . .

CAMMILLO.

Indeed! What happened? Do you know that yesterday, heavily stricken with age, Aldobrando your father's friend, died? Among his secret papers were found fervent pleas directed by you to the prince. Tell me: did you really write them?

BEATRICE.

What you are asking!

CAMMILLO.

Open your whole heart to me. Reveal every secret to your friend Cammillo. Then don't fear that anything said will be spread about.

BEATRICE.

Oh unfortunate me! Will I have to reopen the mortal wound? It must be eight months since I wrote them.

CAMMILLO.

Oh heaven! The papers were withheld by design. He didn't have them before this morning.

BEATRICE.

Oh it is clear now that Aldobrando was my father's friend! What did the Prince tell you?

CAMMILLO.

Ah Beatrice! I saw that holy old man weep over your papers. With the loudest voice I heard him denounce Aldobrando.

BEATRICE.

He did not say a word to you about my papers?

CAMMILLO.

He did not; and I would have asked too much. No one overhears us: your confiding in me goes deep into my heart. Your firm friend, your true friend is very anxious to hear from your lips . . . .

BEATRICE.

Oh God! What a pass you have come to, O Beatrice! After having given me the calm I sought you are forcing from me the great secret that I believed might die with the prince. A noble, stable friend like you is not to be found, and you deserve my explaining everything to you. Hear me then: four years ago today I saw my tender mother go down into her grave. My father's deeds were the cause. Although I was young in years, I saw everything, I learned everything with great revulsion. He was the tyrant of his days. His evil genius has not died out yet. I grew up in the midst of shameful goings-on. Wicked women often were close to me. I saw things which uprightness flees from telling, and does not find words for. When I became an adult, what was I to resolve? To you my great friend I never wanted to tell anything: the wise man flees from the house of the wicked; you alone were my comfort. What was I to do? Humbly at my father's feet, I beg him to change his ways. And finally I tell him that the time had come when marriage might take me away. An enemy hears more easily from a hostile adversary a worse design. He confines me: he even cuts me off from the air, and he wants to deprive me even more. . . . Ah Sir, pardon me! Ah my Cammillo! You excellent man, highest in sensibilities, generous man, don't ask of me anything else, don't force from me what nature itself, very nature would be ashamed of.

CAMMILLO.

Where is that heart so firm that it does not dissolve into tears at your telling? Here is the reason for your supplications, here is the terrible outcome of the delay.

BEATRICE.

I begged life of the holy old man: I begged him that he should soon take me away from my father's cruel power. That reduced to a low maidservant, he would give me as a gift to someone. That he should put me where true souls are who are taken from the noise of the world; in a tomb worse than if I were a guilty vestal; that in sum he should uproot me from that horrible life of death.

CAMMILLO.

Your martyrdoms are mine. I am discovering the great necessity that drove you to a virtuous step that honors you; and I am discovering all the baleful vicissitudes to which the purest reputation is subject. Now I do not desire to hear from you what it was that happened afterwards to that deadly man. I hope you have not forgotten that he was your father in spite of his evil mind: in a few moments I will see you again: I am returning to the Sovereign . . . but first I would like to see Marsilio. . . .

BEATRICE.

You are leaving me? This is your way of consoling me?

CAMMILLO.

Beatrice! Time is precious now. Still appeal to and implore the help of courage. May nature, the need of staying alive, the evidence of your reason raise your spirit to the highest degree, reinvigorate it; may they restore you to your youth, to your sex, to the world no object of guilt but a luminous example of virtue.

FAUSTO, BEATRICE, CAMMILLO.

FAUSTO.

The Judge is coming, O woman . . .

CAMMILLO.

Just now . . .

FAUSTO.

How do you happen to be here?

CAMMILLO.

Read.

(Presenting to him a sheet of paper.)

FAUSTO.

I humbly submit to the order.

CAMMILLO.

I want to see the Judge . . .

FAUSTO.

Sir, I offer myself as your guide.

BEATRICE.

Return to me: think of the state I am left in.

CAMMILLO.

Fear not: in the meantime calm your soul. Noble valor conquers fate, avenges insults, and restores oppressed innocence to its pure state.

End of the Third Act

ACT IV

Scene i

MARSILIO, FAUSTO.

MARSILIO.

Let Beatrice be called and the others likewise advance at the same time . . . Ah Fausto! I fear that today may be a black day for them.

FAUSTO.

Heaven takes care that the unworthy should always be caught by snares.

Scene ii

MARSILIO, *then* BEATRICE.

MARSILIO.

Here is the woman. She seems completely unconnected with the ways of perfidy. But such great and such definite suspicions arise, deadly accusations, voices and tears against her that make her guilty without any defense. I am a firm judge. . . . Sit down, young lady. I eliminated public attendance from the procedure; a private case. . . .

BEATRICE.

As you wish. I have no fear of the presence of Rome.

MARSILIO.

At least your spirit may sustain your innocence. Meanwhile you endure the fateful countenance of those who call you guilty of a black crime.

Scene iii

FAUSTO *and Soldiers, who escort* MARZIO *and* OLIMPIO *in chains.*

BEATRICE, MARSILIO.

FAUSTO.

Here at your order are the wicked men, Sir.

MARZIO.

What do I see! O stars! Beatrice!

OLIMPIO.

Allow me . . . . I want to see . . . .

MARSILIO.

Keep quiet. Let truth, always suspect in the mouth of the guilty, be now the salvation of the upright. The common weakness put all of us on the brink of falling. Lucky the one who does not go off the straight path and becomes a wise model for the others! First calm your heart if it beats fast; then start by telling us your name.

OLIMPIO.

I will answer. We were once servants of Francesco: my name is Olimpio. . . .

MARZIO.

I am Marzio.

MARSILIO.

What most strange motive drove you to flight?

OLIMPIO.

A grave danger.

MARSILIO.

Explain yourself clearly.

OLIMPIO.

We will. At a servant's peformance of a task, our Master, who had a deadly disposition, was accustomed quite often to give us knocks and blows. We lived the life of animals.

MARSILIO.

And what? You could not go with another master?

OLIMPIO.

On the contrary we had made up our minds.

MARSILIO.

And who held up your plan?

OLIMPIO.

It was Beatrice. Young lady, you so wise, so sweet, so loving to us, forgive us. Nature bids all to defend themselves.

MARSILIO.

Make the story clear.

OLIMPIO.

Willingly. When we wanted to leave, she came to us. An isolated girl, desperate girl, filled with anguish, always subjected to a wicked father; where could she find for herself a restraint that could hold her back. She put a knife in our hands, saying there is no other means, means more ready than this, whence to remove us from the common tyranny.

MARSILIO.

Beatrice! Are they telling the truth?

BEATRICE.

I hardly remember these people.

MARSILIO.

They were not your servants?

BEATRICE.

They might have been.

MARSILIO.

Whatever am I hearing? Can you deny what all Rome knows?

BEATRICE.

And let Rome know it; why was a young woman supposed to know servants?

MARSILIO.

Continue.

OLIMPIO.

Oh we are really unfortunate if the lady continues to be obstinate about the truth! You do not recognize us?

BEATRICE.

My never having even a slight memory of it rules out any acquaintance with you.

OLIMPIO.

My courage is beginning to weaken.

MARZIO.

Olimpio, be careful, don't get confused. What will become of us?

OLIMPIO.

We are being truthful in everything. She gave us the knife. The night had descended in silence, and where Francesco's soul lay sleeping in the glow of a dim lamp she made us go in. At that sight she screamed: strike.

MARSILIO.

She gave you the knife?

OLIMPIO.

The woman.

MARSILIO.

Let's look at the knife.

OLIMPIO.

Were we supposed perhaps to keep on us the cruel instrument of crime?

MARSILIO.

Here is the dagger. Examine it carefully.

MARZIO.

Ah Olimpio, what did you say! The dagger was mine, we don't want to lie; and I affirm that this is the one. In the manger where as keeper I first fed the warhorses I used it in lowly toil.

OLIMPIO.

Who can erase the mistake now?

MARSILIO.

What subdued voices! . . . Tremble, wicked!

MARZIO.

I will speak. I do not seek to avoid death. There is no evil design in me. I want to tell the whole and pure truth. Olimpio's deception was in maintaining that the young lady brought it to us in her hand.

MARSILIO.

Treachery conceals itself in vain. A guilty beginning! Continue.

OLIMPIO.

Here I am . . .

MARZIO.

Olimpio, let me tell it; I see the matter clearly.

OLIMPIO.

And I too; don't doubt it. At that sight of our drowsy master, pity seized us to our hearts. He so alone and defenseless, we strong and armed; in that condition we did not wish in any way to put him to death.

MARSILIO.

And why did you kill him?

OLIMPIO.

The bold young woman took the knife from our hands, and

full of a fury as guilty as unexpected, rushed to the bed to strike, screaming you ought to learn spirit from a woman! Such a rebuke struck us in the heart, stirring up cruel frenzies: and we made fierce more by her desire than by ours, with three mortal stabs took the soul from his body; and the young lady, still raging, again snatched the knife from my hand, and on the dead body thumped a blow.

MARSILIO.

Let's verify about Francesco. *(He takes some sheets and reads.)* He died wounded by three strokes. The fourth was not there.

MARZIO.

Let me speak. You don't recall well how it went. Beatrice did not put her hand to the deed.

MARSILIO.

As betrayers! Is this the way you keep the fatal misdeed sorted out in your mind? Where can we find anyone who can learn from you what the truth is? Who can distinguish innocence from crime? Well then, you to whom, by whom, memory better bears witness, and who holds honesty in esteem, continue the story.

MARZIO.

Fear invades my heart . . . but courage . . . oh I search it in vain within me! . . . one must have it here.

MARSILIO.

Are you trembling?

MARZIO.

No, no: only that in the telling Olimpio was mistaken, as I said. . . .

MARSILIO.

I am not wrong. You for certain are more guilty than he; but the fear in your heart betrays you.

MARZIO.

Ah no! please let me tell it all: I am revealing the truth. After Beatrice made us guilty of the evil deed, and at the same time could show herself a daring and wicked daughter, in order to cover her savage and vile crime, she committed to us the dead

body that from the balcony . . . where a ravine slopes down
. . . oh poor me! I have no more breath . . . my voice and heart
tremble.

MARSILIO.

Nefarious! so you tried to lessen your guilt?

MARZIO.

I'm lost. . . . Olimpio, you go on, don't be disheartened. . . .

OLIMPIO.

I have cold fear in my heart: I see no escape.

MARZIO.

Escape this mantle here may give us. Do you see it?

BEATRICE.

I see it.

MARSILIO.

Whom did this mantle belong to?

MARZIO.

Ask the young lady about it.

BEATRICE.

It was a mantle belonging to my father. . . .

MARSILIO.

Who gave it to you?

MARZIO.

Beatrice gave it. Can you deny it? How could one acquire it,
how without you?

BEATRICE.

Look at the scoundrels! Was it perchance difficult for those
who took away my father's life with so much cunning and
fury to take away from him a mantle?

MARZIO.

I can't stand any more. I see the ground spinning. My heart
has betrayed me . . . I feel the tremors of death.

OLIMPIO.

My mind can stand no more. . . . Marzio . . . .

MARZIO.

If no defense remains for us any longer, at least let us try to
save Beatrice.

MARSILIO.

The wicked have finally been capable of remorse. What are

80

you saying? Is any other way left for you? Who has ever seen a more confused villain than you!

MARZIO.

And whom has divine justice not reached! Truth triumphs. Sir, we will now bare our soul to you: desperation, cruel hatred, desire of revenge, which in the heart of servants is strong, drove us to the misdeed. Francesco was so fierce of manner and strange with his people that none may ever hope to match him. We passed our days then from such tribulation to tribulation that fierce desire armed our criminal hand against our cruel master. With this man dead we thought we would be happy. Beatrice was our idol; her gentle heart, her pure virtue, her great and noble soul silently promised us every good thing. But guilt does not reap happiness: heaven is just. We had scarcely consummated the terrible misdeed than cruel remorse and fear were tormenting us. We saw written everywhere our horrible sentence, and we feared that everyone might know our crime. In this horrible, atrocious struggle of continual suffering we resolved to leave those walls where the blood still was coagulated, that blood that we had shed . . . oh God! execute upon us the terrible command. Do not spare deserved death to the iniquitous.

OLIMPIO.

We ask it of you, we beg it; to us life has become an unsupportable burden.

MARSILIO.

Go: the fate which awaits you you will hear.

    Marzio and Olimpio are led away.)

Young lady, you are free. May Rome now know the happy event. Let liberty be granted at once to her servants.

(He goes out with Fausto and the soldiers.)

Scene iv

CAMMILLO, BEATRICE

CAMMILLO.
> And will it be true, Beatrice, that I may clasp you innocent to my heart? Oh now everything has changed all at once! . . . What is it? You don't look happy.

BEATRICE.
> Oh my Cammillo! My heart is so besieged by so many emotions that I am almost going out of my mind.

CAMMILLO.
> Great is the proof that you have given. Now it is finally right to clear from your heart the remembrance of the bitter misfortunes.

BEATRICE.
> Ah peace is far removed from me. Eternal sadness comes near me.

CAMMILLO.
> O Beatrice! I will have accomplished nothing if I cannot take you away from these walls. Set your heart to leave the dark sight of Rome, where for you memories are alive of so much misery. Let us go to the bank of the Arno, where heaven so favorably shines on art and learning. Let us go where the Adige and the Po fertilize the pleasant, fruitful countryside. We will cross the cold Alps, and the deep valleys which the Rhone divides. We will then look upon the Spanish sea, we will gaze upon the Seine, and everything that you will want most. I beg you to agree to my desire. I speak with experience on my side. The dark mood that the fate of Eleanora produced in me, of Eleanora my beloved wife, disappeared at the vista of the foreign shores that I was telling you about.

BEATRICE.
> A terrible ghost holds my feet and heart in chains: I cannot leave Rome.

CAMMILLO.
> What are you saying? I want to comfort you.

BEATRICE.

You ask an impossible thing: it is the will of heaven that I live in sorrow.

End of the Fourth Act.

ACT V

Scene i

BEATRICE, FAUSTO

FAUSTO.

The guilty ask to speak with you. Young lady, to show yourself deaf to the request would be a commendable deed. Think of the crime they are guilty of. An evil desire impels them before you, and they seek a desperate protection from punishment. You will see that with the excesses of a tormented conscience they will give vent to an immense false sorrow, they will dissolve in tears to draw you to the blameworthy step of begging mercy for them. The decision of the Judge is now final that condemns them both to death.

BEATRICE.

I know it, and know also that the wicked have their rights. It is true that a daughter whose father was barbarously murdered by them ought not to yield to pleas, ought not feel pity in her heart. But if we think that a brief instant can take away prudence and reason from the wise, we can tolerate the presence of the guilty without diminishing the punishment. The passions were given us from heaven for our life and for our torment. The guilty has always the right to be heard. See to it that immediately they may come forward in private.

Scene ii

BEATRICE.

> We exist without knowing who we are . . . . Oh profoundest mystery of nature, that puts us in hope, in fear, and never does day return that does not give vigor to hope and to fear. Here they are. I am in the saddest circumstance to which horrible fate can lead.

Scene iii

MARZIO, OLIMPIO *simply chained*, BEATRICE

BEATRICE.

> What do you want?

MARZIO.

> Sentence of blood was pronounced on us. Death will be intolerable, young lady, if first we could not be granted to present to you our wishes and misfortunes.

BEATRICE.

> I am listening.

MARZIO.

> We die now, young lady; there is no hope. At least we will die with fearless heart, both of us, since our death saves you. Before us there are no longer judges. We can present openly the feelings of our souls. Your father had a secret death, and he would have had it publicly, an abominable death, if he had been born poor. Often we see granted to the powerful what is denied to the common man . . . But what good is it to talk of useless things. I leave, Beatrice, a beloved mother, who is bent by her eightieth year. Since my departure a month ago today I haven't had news of her. The so good and unfortunate old woman will be enveloped in poverty. I supported her with leftovers that I could draw from this generous household. In the midst of tears, if by chance she lives still, she will be unhappy because of my flight. Console her, you who are

so generous, and ready to alleviate those who live in misfortune; have some help reach her. At least, if heaven still wantts
her alive, don't let poverty kill her.

BEATRICE.

What is her name?

(Drying her eyes with a handkerchief.)

MARZIO.

Fabia.

BEATRICE.

Does Lorenzo know her?

MARZIO.

Certainly.

BEATRICE.

And you ask nothing?

OLIMPIO.

Beatrice! I find myself completely without relatives. I wish
for my part to lay down my life for you, without the least
profit.

BEATRICE.

But be calm of spirit; you will not die.

MARZIO.

What! . . . Listen, young lady. The best work that the universe can look for from us, from us humble folk, never stops,
and, always in the midst of contempt is spontaneous death.

OLIMPIO.

We are resolved; we are strong; we are really tranquil.

BEATRICE.

Go: after a little you will hear something about me. *(They go
out.)*

Scene iv

FAUSTO, BEATRICE.

FAUSTO.

All the servants wish to see you, O Beatrice.

BEATRICE.

Don't let any of them hold back. . . . *(The Servants of each sex come forward.)* Oh good people! Oh how much it pains me to have disturbed you.

THE MEN.

Ah take them! Consecrated to you be the tears of immense joy that we shed.

THE WOMEN.

We are returned to new life. . . .

BEATRICE.

I want to provide for your future wellbeing. Lorenzo! Let there be for everyone bread for life; and may he lose, if he wishes, the status of servant.

THE MEN.

Oh God! What are you saying, young lady! What spirit will we have after all, we are dedicated to you?

THE WOMEN.

Don't give us this sorrow. What good is life without you?

BEATRICE.

Don't go on: my heart is drowning in tears. Listen: also let Fabia, disconsolate mother of Marzio, have generous assistance. . . . Oh my Teresa! You will remain. I will see you others again. *(The servants leave making signs of the most extreme sorrow.)* Bring me a goblet of the purest water. It will give relief to my weak heart. *(Teresa executes the order.)* I am to live!

Stained thus in the sweet April of life? . . . I don't have clear ideas; reflection does not guide my confused mind. . . . And this is the bosom where the virtues are reposed? . . . Virtue in me? . . . *(Teresa returns with a glass full of water.)* Leave it. . . . Teresa! Embrace me. Hold me to your heart . . . I have recognized your rare fidelity. Your fortune will no longer be moderate. . . . Oh God! To what purpose the anguish? . . . A happy face! We all must disappear. Go. . . .

(Teresa leave weeping uncontrollably.)

Who protects honor, which flies! who horror, infamy, which come on rapidly! . . . Here is the great means.

(Brings out a little cartridge.)
Tremble, O Fathers, if you don't fulfil your duty to your children. . . .
    (She pours into the glass the poison which was in the cartridge.)
Here is what children come to . . .
    (She drinks.)
Alas! I will not be living in an hour. . . . Do not make me tremble, guilty soul! The moment of truth has finally come . . . What is it?

Scene v

IPPOLITO, BEATRICE

IPPOLITO.
    Beatrice, I am beside myself with pleasure.
BEATRICE.
    Tender Friend! Here finally is the desired and so much hoped-for moment. . . .
IPPOLITO.
    My heart leaps! . . . Oh happy me! and it will be true?
BEATRICE.
    Lorenzo! *(Lorenzo comes in.)*
        I want to talk to Marsilio.

Scene vi

MARSILIO, BEATRICE, IPPOLITO, *then* CAMMILLO.

MARSILIO.
    Before your call I was coming to you.
CAMMILLO.
    Beatrice! the holy Old Man rejoices with you, and gives us the freedom to abandon the afflicted confines of the country.

Nothing else remains for you but immediately to jump on the vehicle: all is in readiness. Have your Teresa come and Lorenzo. I hope to see you happy under a new sky.

BEATRICE.

Quite a different desire is in my heart . . . Cammillo! . . .

CAMMILLO.

Your voice surprises me.

BEATRICE.

Alas! I do not wish to be forever against the truth; listen at last to my words of extreme revulsion. First, Sir, commute the penalty of the guilty. . . .

MARSILIO.

What are you saying!

BEATRICE.

They are not so guilty as they make themselves, miserable ones! The desire was not in them to take my father's life.

MARSILIO.

And whose was it?

BEATRICE.

Whatever are you looking for? . . . Allow the case to remain forever buried in eternal oblivion.

MARSILIO.

But justice . . .

BEATRICE.

What is justice! . . . What has justice done about the operations of a perfidious man? . . . Ah what am I saying? He was my father; didn't he give me life? I am the guilty one. . . . Forgive me! A heart that is so full of sorrow overflows.

CAMMILLO.

I don't understand her. . . .

IPPOLITO.

O wretched me!

MARSILIO.

Explain yourself.

BEATRICE.

Yes, we will not see justice insulted. You will see fall before the altar a victim so contrite. . . .

CAMMILLO.

You are raving, O Beatrice. . . . Love your life. . . .

BEATRICE.

I can't . . . Oh God! Can life diminish the cause of my tears? I have lost every right to life. Nothing remains for me but the succor of heaven. Instead of producing on earth one like me, nature would do better, it would do better to remain sterile for a hundred years.

CAMMILLO.

Hey, get up! . . .

IPPOLITO.

Come out of your madness!

CAMMILLO.

The confines of your home fill your heart with sad thoughts. . . . They make you think cruel things.

BEATRICE.

I have a soul so depressed that I no longer see anything clearly.

CAMMILLO.

I am willing. In spite of everything I want to take you away.

BEATRICE.

But where could I show myself, I a desperate woman, to snatch even from the flowers the grateful odor, to roll the most limpid wave, to poison the air you breathe? I am beside myself. . . . Teresa! hurry . . .

(Teresa comes in, runs up to her, and sustains her.)

The sun this morning rose so black, but a more fearful night will descend with anger and blood. . . . Nature takes revenge.

. . .

CAMMILLO.

And who can endure the fateful scene?

IPPOLITO.

Beatrice certainly took powerful poison . . . and this is the goblet. . . . Look at the black bottom!

MARSILIO.

Here is evident the real guilt.

BEATRICE.

Oh children, by my example . . . learn to tolerate any pater-
nal crime however atrocious . . . you fathers . . . ah enough!
. . . who can impose heavy servitude to equal my father's?
Heaven shows a happy look . . . . The air is becoming more
beautiful. . . . Who would believe it? . . . Even the shapeless
mass . . . . The whole creation rejoices at my death.

End.

Beatrice Cenci.

Beatrice.
Cammillo.
Ippolito.
Marsilio.
Fausto.
Marzio.
Olimpio.
Soldati.

Servi.
Serve

di Beatice.

La scena è in Roma in casa di Beatrice.

ATTO PRIMO.

Scena i.

CAMILLO, BEATRICE.

CAMMILLO.
> Liberi sensi, a chi per te nel petto
> Di verace amistà conserva il nome,
> Beatrice, esponi. Non saria il silenzio
> Che intempestivo o insolito riguardo.
> Roma divenne, ben lo veggo, stanza
> D'orrido lutto. Riposata un'ora
> Passar non puoi, dove il terribil fato
> Dell'infelice Padre tuo risuona
> Sulle labbra di tutti. Omai solleva
> L'abbattute sembianze, e ti risolvi
> D'abbandonare questo suol. Tua scorta
> M'offro secura. L'età mia tutt'ora
> Per natura viril, ma che al gran peso
> Del già compito sessantesimo anno
> Sta per piegare, il non ignobil grido
> Della mia fama, libera ti fanno
> Dai giudizj del Mondo. I tristi mali
> Spesso si vincon col variar di terra,
> Coll'osservar regni e provincie, usanze
> E costumi novelli. Io che per prova
> Lo so, tel dico. L'esperienza, a cui
> Proprio si rendo il salutar consiglio,
> Sol per tuo ben la mia favella sprona.

BEATRICE.
> Dall'opre tue, da' liberali modi
> Limpida appare sempre più l'invitta
> Farnesia stirpe. Nel mio cor ben dentro
> Scolpita sempre l'amistrà tua saggia
> Sarà, o Cammillo. Il tuo cortese invito
> Dovria accettar, dovria fuggir da questo
> Cielo fatale, e non tornar più mai . . . .

92

Misera! ... ah, dove andar potrò, che meco
La mia pena crudel sempre non tragga!
CAMMILLO.
  Ha i confini il dolor. Forse siam nati
  Per vivere nel pianto? ova'è quell'alma,
  A cui morte rapir non abbia osato
  Qualche tenero oggetto! Il tempo vince
  Non solamente le memorie avverse,
  Ma le propizie ancor. Lo so che atroce
  Il fine fu del Padre tuo, non anche
  Dalla natura stabilito, e merta
  Più lacrime filiali; e pur l'alzarsi
  Dall'incessante doglia tua non fora
  Sola virtude, ma dover richiesto
  Dall'obbligo di vita.
BEATRICE.
                      Assai comprendo
  Il naturale mio dover. Vorrei
  Vincer l'affanno, romper la sorgente
  Dell'immagini meste; respirare
  Aure grate, cessar dal pianto in somma.
  Ma, Signore, non posso: il duol mio fiero
  Superabil non è.
CAMMILLO.
                  Cagion mai fora
  Del tua dolore la memoria trista
  Che lasciò in Roma il Padre tuo? l'orgoglio
  Con cui talor l'opere sue vestiva,
  E il prepotente genio suo feroce
  Come scusar? figlia amorosa troppo
  Eri d'un padre scostumato: dirlo
  È forza omai. Nel dirupato scoglio
  Chi lo guidava? Ragionevol spirto
  Corse giammai di precipizj in traccia?
  Trarti da queste sconsolate mura
  Voglio, Beatrice. I voti miei seconda;
  Non ti ostinar; renderti un Padre io bramo.
  Lo stesso Ciel, se nel tuo volto pose

Gentilezza, contegno e rara idea,
Danna l'inutil tua tristezza.
BEATRICE.

Io sono

Si, nell'ira del Ciel. . . .
CAMMILLO.

Ma come! quale

Può averci mal senza rimedio? dimmi,
Te molestar potrebbe Amor? . . . Pur fosse. . . .
Amor colpevol non sarà. . . . mi svela
L'anima tua; qui alcun non ci ode: parla
È ignobile il tuo amante? Anima vile
Creder nol posso. Stai tranquilla: ho mezzi
Per dargli grado. Dinne il nome.
BEATRICE.

Ah mio

Tenero Amico! . . . ma chi avanza ratto! . . .
CAMMILLO.

Ippolito mi par . . . ma di'. . . .
BEATRICE.

Deh amore

Non m'angustia, o Cammillo! Avvi pur troppo
Chi nasce alla sventura. Avvi chi lieto
Esser non deve mai . . . Che fia? . . .

Scena ii

IPPOLITO, BEATRICE, CAMMILLO.

IPPOLITO.

Novelle

Incredibili reco . . . . Oh tempi! i sacri
Recessi dove hanno riposo l'Ombre
Più securi non son. Avvi chi ardisce
Con scarilega man dal quieto avello
Trarre la spoglia di tu Padre . . . .

94

BEATRICE.
                    Oh lassa!
     Che narri tu? . . . Il tremore della morte
     Tutte le membra m'agita.
CAMMILLO.
                    Qual dassi
     Ragion dell'opra?
IPPOLITO.
                    Del Sovrano in mente
     Feri sospetti entraro. Egli non crede
     Che Francesco infuriato, disperato,
     Non men che privo di ragion, potesse
     Della sua casa da un balcon lanciarsi
     Nella rupe profonda. Anzi temendo,
     Che ciò non fosse perfidissim'arte
     Di chi la vita con furor gli tolse,
     Ora fa il corpo esaminar.
BEATRICE.
                    Comanda,
     Chi regna ancora sugli estinti?
CAMMILLO.
                    Sai
     Del cenno i resultati?
IPPOLITO.
                    Appena il corpo
     Fuori fu della tomba, ebbi desìo
     Di correre a Beatrice.
BEATRICE.
                    E le vive aure
     Non rifuggir sdegnate dalla fredda
     Spoglia? Rea notte non coperse a un tratto
     Il sacro asilo profanato? Il Cielo
     Non fulminò sopra l'avverse mani
     Accinte all'opra? . . . e viver deggio? e deggio
     Viver lieta, o Cammillo!
CAMMILLO.
                    Orrido è il fatto:

Ma di chi regna il vigilar, Beatrice,
Soverchio non fu mai. Chi sa che giusto
Il sospetto non sia? Chi sa che il caso
Non abbia offerto un evidente indizio
Di Francesco sul fato? è ver, ch'egli era
Arrogante, intrattabile, superbo;
Dannoso agli altri, di natura un male,
E grave a se .... Ma chi ragione al mondo
Di sua morte può dar? Qualche suo fiero
Destro nemico arditamente infino
Nell'interna magion, chi sa, che il piede
Inoltrato non abbia? e qual valore
Per trucidar uomo nel sonno o colto
All'improvviso? Indi malizia somma
Insegna il fallo a ricoprir. La rupe
Eravi all'uopo.
BEATRICE.
                    Che mai narri? Dove
Stavamo noi? ... Ma, oh ferità di cose! ...
Basta, succeder tutto può, siccome
Tutto si dà per rendermi l'oggetto
Della natura il più infelice .... Bramo
De'miei tristi pensier sola un istante
Restare in preda. Perfettissim'alma
Sta in te, o Cammillo. Non vorrei lasciarti
Che per quel poco. Ippolito tu pure
I passi siegui dell'Amico e quindi
Ritornate ... ma no ... che ardisco! Sete
Seguaci troppo di virtù illibata.
Misera tanto femmina qual sono
Pregio non ho per obbligarvi ... oh Dio!
Ed è possibil ch'io virtù discacci? ...
Ah il veggo ben! dolor non vi ha che uccida.
IPPOLITO.
Empirti il cor di filial ribrezzo
Tal novella dovea. Son di giustizia
Però liberi i passi, e ormai conviene

L'atto assoluto tollerar . . . . Ascolto
Gente appressarsi. . . .
CAMMILLO.
Militari in armi! . . .

Scena iii

FAUSTO *con seguito di Soldati,* BEATRICE, CAMMILLO,
IPPOLITO.

BEATRICE.
A che venite?
FAUSTO.
Sei Beatrice?
BEATRICE.
Il sono.
FAUSTO.
Sollecita adunar fa'di tua Casa
Tutti i servi e l'ancelle. Onde partirne
Attenderete l'ordin voi. . . . Soldati,
Tutti gl'ingressi custodite.
BEATRICE.
Avrai
Sovrano cenno?
FAUSTO.
Arbitrio no. A tua voglia
Veder lo puoi.
BEATRICE.
Non più. Lorenzo! aduna
Tosto di Casa la servil mia gente;
Qui la conduci.
(Lorenzo escirà nel momento.)
IPPOLITO.
Qual proceder!
CAMMILLO.
Pena

Mortal, che in cor di Beatrice piomba,
Questa misura è certo. Io non comprendo
Tanto rigore. La fortuna avversa
Pone a prova gli Amici. Odi: io mi rendo
Mallevador di tutti . . . .

FAUSTO.

Alto è il comando;
Ceder non posso ad alcun patto.

CAMMILLO.

Almeno
Non tacerne il motivo.

BEATRICE.

E quando fosse
Causa di ciò malvagità segreta,
Chi ripara all'onor?

FAUSTO.

A tutto para
La scoperta innocenza.

BEATRICE.

E chi reprime
Lo spavento dell'alma?

FAUSTO.

Ove spavento,
Senza delitto?

BEATRICE.

Avvi dell'alme, in cui
Onde il timor spesso fatal non entri,
L'innocenza non serve.

FAUSTO.

Ognor costume
Di Magistrato non fallevol fia,
Dell'opra assicurarsi.

BEATRICE.

Alberga quivi
La colpa?

FAUSTO.

Io servo al cenno.

BEATRICE.

Ebben; ti prendi
Libertà qual ti aggrada, ecco i miei servi.
*(Escono Uomini e Donne appartenenti al servizio di
Beatrice.)*

FAUSTO.

Un d'ogni sesso fra di loro eleggi:
Regoli il genio tuo la scelta.

BEATRICE.

E gli altri?

FAUSTO.

Saran securi; non temer.

BEATRICE.

Vo'prima
Saper la sorte di ciascun.

FAUSTO.

Tranquilla
Farti non posso.

BEATRICE.

Ebben, Teresa resti
Meco, e Lorenzo. Dimmi; avrò balia
Di provveder chi va?

FAUSTO.

Sta in te.

BEATRICE.

Lorenzo,
Prendi *(Gli dà una chiave.)* . . . fortuna a me nego la pace;
Oro non già: di questo a lor qual vuoi
Somma, puoi dare generosa. Intendi,
Dove son tratti: a me il dirai tu poscia.

FAUSTO.

Ola! scortate questa gente; e voi. . . .

CAMMILLO.

Parlar ne lascia! Me conosce Roma,
Me il Sovran ben conosce. In me non cape
Pensier di colpa, nè magion frequento
Amica del delitto. Or su: m'estimo

Degno d'intender, di saper qual sia
Di questo severissimo apparato
La causa. Bramo riparar di tanti
L'onor, la tema. Facoltadi e posse
Grandi in me stanno. Non mi oppongo a legge,
Nè la converto. Sol vorrei che il tanto
Pubblico dire s'evitasse.

FAUSTO.
                    Udiste?
Tu in miglior tempo il tuo gran cor palesa.

Fine dell'Atto Primo.

ATTO SECONDO.

Scena i.

IPPOLITO, BEATRICE.

IPPOLITO.
          Più me stesso non trovo. A che qui stretti
          Siamo da gente di pietà deserta,
          Colma d'ogni rigor? Beatrice, oh Dio!
          Che possiamo temer? forse dal freddo
          Corpo del Padre tuo segni scuopriro,
          Da cui ne insorgan tai severi modi?
          Io non ho pace. Udii di più poc'anzi
          Che arrestar fuor di Roma ambo i tuoi servi
          Marzio e Olimpio spariti.

BEATRICE.
                    Olimpio e Marzio
          Arrestaro?

IPPOLITO.
                    Costor da te involati,

Dopo il successo lacrimabil caso,
Sospetto diero, come sai, nè un giorno
Cessò giustizia d'inseguirli. Alfine
Giunti, chi sa, che confession mendace
Della lor fuga non facesser? Quindi
Ecco a buon grado esaminarsi il corpo,
Ecco a buon grado sveller della tomba
L'aride spoglie di Francesco. Il fero
Atto pensando poi ch'era in tua casa
Stato adempito, ecco il rigor per tutti,
Eccoci tutti nel sospetto involti . . . .
Ma che avvenne, o Beatrice? eri più mesta
Pria di saper queste novelle. Ammiro
Del tuo cor la fermezza. I casi amari
Fan distinguer gli spirti, e la contanza
Supera l'odio della sorte avversa.

BEATRICE.

Lieta però non son. Mi scende in petto
A torrenti la pena; e giunte agli occhi
Mi s'impiertran le lacrime . . . . Cammillo,
Dimmi, ove sta? Perchè da me nol veggo?

IPPOLITO.

Tutto attento scrivea; verrà a momenti . . . .
Oh trista sorte di nostr'alme! Quando
L'Imen più dolce stringer le potea,
Che la virtù, che la natura a gara
Prodotto avesser mai . . . .

BEATRICE.

           Taci: non farmi
Quella repressa mia fatale angoscia
Scoppiare in pianto, o in spasimi di morte.
Amor, che incontro a mia crescente etade
Farsi leggiadro e caro ognor vedea,
Sparì dagli occhi miei. Dovunque io vada,
L'aure per me diventan tosco. Un'ora
Non ho di pace. Sulle piume stresse,
Vedove sempre di tranquillo sonno,
Non porto che gli affanni . . . . Ah no! d'affanni

Più non parliam. Nè tu irritar co'detti
Oppresso cor . . . Tempo è d'ardir. Si pensi
La mia fama a coprir dai crudi assalti
Del nemico destino. . . . Ola! chi avanza?
Chiama Cammillo subito.

Scena ii.

MARSILIO, BEATRICE

MARSILIO.
                    Sarai
     Beatrice.
BEATRICE.
                         Lo dicesti.
MARSILIO.
                              Or via; t'avvezza
     A sostener di Giudice incorrotto
     La severa presenza. Alcun non tema
     Pria del delitto. Questo error dell'uomo,
     Di rea passion figlio primiero e padre,
     L'uomo avvili. . . . Ma che ragiono! Tanto
     Tu così ornata di celesti forme
     Puoi conoscer delitti? All crudele
     Necessità dona il disturbo adunque.
     Senza tema rispondimi. La gente
     Tua dove sta?
BEATRICE.
                    Cenno la tolse. Due
     Sol rimaser de'miei.
MARSILIO.
                         Va ben. Teresa
     L'una, l'altro Lorenzo *(Tacitamente osservando un
     foglio, che avrà seco.)* Ancor vi sono
     Due . . .
BEATRICE.
                    D'amistà . . . .

102

MARSILIO.

       Tu il di': *(Seguitando a leggere*
come sopra.)   Cammil Farnese.
Ed Ippolito Guerra. Ti ritira
Nella prossima stanza, e qui s'inoltri
Cammil.

Scena iii.

CAMMILLO, MARSILIO.

CAMMILLO.

      Da me che cercasi?

MARSILIO.

           Signore!
Amico sei tu di virtù cotanto,
Che non ho cor di fingerti per ombra
Nemmeno reo.

CAMMILLO.

        Parla: tuo posto cuopri
Senza riguardi.

MARSILIO.

       Mi convien. La salda
Legge a tutti li toglie. Dimmi: è molto
Che tu conosci Beatrice?

CAMMILLO.

            Crebbe
Fra le mie braccia.

MARSILIO.

      Un'amistà sol ferma
Ti conducea sempre a vederla?

CAMMILLO.

          Voglia
Non altra mai.

MARSILIO.

      Tu di mentir capace,

Signor, non sei. La libertà, che accorda
La tua magion, prendi per ora.
CAMMILLO.

                      Ascolta. . . .

MARSILIO.
    Signor, perdona. D'ubbidire è tempo,
Non di parole. Il caso è fier. Soldati,
Siategli scorta.
CAMMILLO.

                     Grazia chiedo. Resti
La guida. Io con Ippolito trarrommi
Alla mia casa.
MARSILIO.

          Debbo edirlo.
CAMMILLO.

                 Poscia
Far lo potrai. Ti sia di lui garante
la mia sacra parola.
MARSILIO.

             Olà, soldati!
Libero passo a Ippolito, a Cammillo
Cedete.

Scena iv.

IPPOLITO, CAMMILLO, MARSILIO.

CAMMILLO.
    Amico, a me t'unisci . . . .
IPPOLITO.

               E addio
Nemmen diremo a Beatrice! . . . Oh specie
Di tormento inaudito!
MARSILIO.

           Alcun più mai
Quivi non entri non chiamato, a trarne
I servi destinati.

CAMMILLO.
>Andiam. Speranza
>Non abbandona i passi miei. Di Roma
>Al Prence ho scritto già: chiedo parlargli:
>Non scorre dì ch'io non lo vegga e l'oda.
>La grazia avrò, sicuro sono: ei stresso
>Mi narrerà quale destino ha resa
>La donzella in cimento.

IPPOLITO.
>Al suo decoro
>La tua pura amistà, Signor, provegga.

Scena v.

MARSILIO.
>Vo'riveder, giacchè costor sen giro,
>L'accusata fanciulla. A me di nuovo
>Si presenti Beatrice. Ancor non posso
>Figurarla così d'empio delitto
>Macchiata; eppur di gran sospetto è rea . . . .
>Pria dell'esame vo'tentar se in parte
>Le scopro il cor. Giovin, com'è, non puote
>Qual uom mostrarsi dalla colpa roso
>Dotto in celar se stesso: e quando fosse
>Innocente davver, vo'consolarla
>E torle ogni timor. Ma s'ella ardita
>Varcato avesse d'ogni dritto il segno,
>Conviene allora il fren tutto disciorre
>A un rigor senza esempio . . . . Eccola.

Scena vi.

BEATRICE, MARSILIO.

MARSILIO.
>Teme

105

Troppo, o Donzella, di nojarti. Ormai
Dato alla legge e al Tribunal, laddove
Porto ferma sembianza a cor tremante,
Mio malgrado molesto esser conviemmi.
La mia presenza non t'ispira in petto
I moti del timor?

BEATRICE.
              Come! vestito
Di ferità sei tu?

MARSILIO.
            Vestito sono
A misura dei casi. Un cor non reo
Mi trova sempre docile. Diverso
La colpa. Udir bramo de te qual merta
Stima un iniquo.

BEATRICE.
            Quella stessa stima,
Che ha in sen chi lo condanna.

MARSILIO.
               Anima saggia
Così risponde. Ilarità chi ha in volto,
Non ha guerra nel petto. Il tuo sembiante
Lieto, mi rassicura. Esservi danno
Può per l'onesto? seguita. D'avversa
Non concepibil crudeltà nemica
Sei fatta scopo. Vincila: disperdi,
Fa' sparire i maligni. Al suon concorde
Delle pubbliche voci eco onorata
Risponderà da' sette colli. Udrai
Di laude gl'inni, e le festose figlie
Di Roma tutte accorreranno in bianche
Vesti, o Beatrice, a rallegrarsi teco.

BEATRICE.
(Si scioglie in dirottiesimo pianto.)

MARSILIO.
Come! tu piangi? . . .

BEATRICE.
           Oh Dio! che fo d'avanti

A si terribil Giudice? . . . Signore,
Non creder no, non creder no che nasca
Da opra pentita il pianto mio.
MARSILIO.
                    Sta' queta
E lo nascondi. Tenerezza immensa,
Desìo d'onor lo muovono. Non sei
Certo tu rea . . . ma strepito s'inalza
Dalle strade di Roma. Ascolto il nome,
Che pronunziano tuo.

Scena vii.

FAUSTO, BEATRICE, MARSILIO.

MARSILIO.
                    Fausto racconta
Dell'improvviso popolar frastuono
I motivi.
FAUSTO.
                Romana ardita gente
Chiede Beatrice di veder. La porta
Da' soldati difesa offre sicura
Dimora quivi.
MARSILIO.
                Vigila, a momenti
S'inoltreran Marzio ed Olimpio. A mia
Richiesta tu li serba.
FAUSTO.
                    Ella sospira;
Oh tardo pentimento!
MARSILIO.
                    E non vi sono
Altre lagrime? . . . Insorgon nuove grida
Guarda, Fausto, e ritorna.

Scena viii.

MARSILIO, BEATRICE.

MARSILIO.
Aver coraggio
Convien, Donzella; sentirai che d'opra
Ti fanno rea, d'opra così, che rompe
Di natura ogni dritto. Io dirtel pria
Voglio, sebben contrario all'uso, affine
Che tu l'alma fortifichi. Il tuo core
Troppo si varia a istanti. Io ti vorrei
Veder sempre un sol volto.
BEATRICE.
Agli apparati
Di colpa io tremo, e dee tremar chi ha l'alma
Nemica della colpa.

Scena ix.

FAUSTO, BEATRICE, MARSILIO.

FAUSTO.
Avvi, Signore,
Cristiano, e Ulisse, illustri genj, e primi
Onor del Foro, e non fallace speme
Di chi lordo apparì di grave accusa.
S'offron spontanei all difesa grande
Della Donna sospetta.
BEATRICE.
(Con gran forza di spirito.)
Io non ho colpa,
Sospetta farmi un traditor sol puote;
Io nulla temo; ergo sicura fronte:
Io non ho d'uopo di sublimi spirti,
Che sostengano gli empj. Avrò talento
Per difendermi io stessa. Io stessa scudo
Farò di me.

108

FAUSTO.

        Ve' qual ardir a un tratto!

MARSILIO.

    Ebben fra un'ora. . . .

BEATRICE.

        Mi vedrai.

MARSILIO.

           T'aspetto.

Fine dell'Atto Secondo.

ATTO TERZO.

Scena i.

FAUSTO, *Sergente.*

FAUSTO.

    Crebbe il rigor. Pria ch'io nol sappia alcuno
    Non passi qui, tranue colui, che avesse
    Cenno Sovran.

Scene ii.

IPPOLITO *travestito*, FAUSTO.

FAUSTO.

        Chi sei?

IPPOLITO.

          Lorenzo,
    Di Beatrice servo.

FAUSTO.

      A te l'ingresso
    Non è vietato.

IPPOLITO.

         Amor, desio fervente
Di giovare alla Donna hanno protetta
La difficil mia impresa.

FAUSTO.

            Odimi. . . .

IPPOLITO.

                Oh cielo!
Ora mi scopre. . . . Che ne chiedi?

FAUSTO.

           A lei
Ti rechi!

IPPOLITO.

      Appunto.

FAUSTO.

         Le dirai che a istanti
L'ora fatale termina.

Scene iii.

BEATRICE, IPPOLITO.

BEATRICE.

        Lorenzo!

IPPOLITO.

Reggiam l'inganno. Beatrice . . . .

BEATRICE.

           Oh voce!
Lorenzo! . . . oh Dio! tu in queste spoglie?

IPPOLITO.

       Il Cielo
Favorì il mio disegno. A ta ne corro
Nunzio di ree novelle. Il tuo decoro,
La tua vita, i tuoi beni in gran periglio
Si veggono. Di te colpevol grido
S'alza per Roma. Non vi ha scampo: dietro

A esame severissimo udirai
Di morte pronunziar cruda sentenza.
Tali feroci avvenimenti e tali
Si accozzarono insiem tremendi casi,
Da non poter difenderti. Il Sovrano
Di Roma freme. Di funesto esempio
Vuol che tu serva a'posteri. Non guardo
Al tuo affano: svelarti il vero anelo.
Salva la vita: poco hai tempo; meco
Verrai. La porta, che segreta guida,
Traversando il giardin, nel vasto circo,
Libera è sempre. Non tardar, risolvi. . . .
Beatrice . . . . oh Ciel! così l'infamia aspetti.
BEATRICE.
Verace amico, Ippolito, verace
Spirito degno! ben ti laudo l'opera;
Non il consiglio, che a seguirlo infamia
Non men di quella, che a restar, m'arriva.
Chi fugge? il vile, o l'anima, che è resa
Fuori di speme, chi ha nel sen la colpa;
Non già chi onor ama, e la vita, e quanto
Di delicato sia nello'universo.
Fero è il cimento. La grandezza tutta
Della sventura mia conosco. L'oro,
I beni immensi, ch'io posseggo, e questa
Mia giovinezza, e di natura i doni
Darei prendendo anche un'età deforme,
E di serva lo stato, onde poterne
Uscire intatta dal feral giudizio.
Pur la speranza, questo ben che mai
Non abbandona chi respira; pure
Un certo cor, che sento in me, non sempre
Tenero in faccia di virtude al nome,
Mi sosterran, valor daranmi. Tutti
Poi corrotti dal tempo, che ci strugge,
Giacerem poca polve. Il fato guida
I nostri piè fino al sepolcro. Noi

Pe' sepolcri viviamo; noi viviamo
Coll'error, che c'invecchia; in mezzo al male
Che dura, e al ben, ch'è un sogno.
IPPOLITO.
                              Beatrice,
Vere cose narrasti; ma talora
La fiducia ne inganna. Un passo ardito
Mai non è quel che salva. Ogni memoria
Il tempo toglie; indi perdiam l'idea
Fin di quello ch'è stato.
BEATRICE.
                         E a che la vita
Senza l'onor! . . .
IPPOLITO.
                    Taci: salvarti io voglio
L'una e l'altro. T'arrendi: il passo ratto
Muovi; ogni istante oro non ha che il paghi.
BEATRICE.
Chi s'avanza?
IPPOLITO.
                    Deh togliti da questo
Fero momento! . . .
BEATRICE.
                  E non lo vedi? Danno
Accrescer posson tue mentite spoglie. . . .
Salva il mio onore, l'onor mio che è posto
In terribile lance. . . . Ah va'l più fassi
Lo strepito vicin.
IPPOLITO.
                   Non vo' lasciarti
In sì grave pericolo . . .
BEATRICE.
                       L'amore
È questo dunque, che hai per me? . . . T'ascondi:
Meco l'istessa verità è sospetta.
IPPOLITO.
Vado, se il vuoi; ma già non lunge: udire
Dell'esame fatal l'esito voglio.

Scena iv.

CAMMILLO, BEATRICE.

CAMMILLO.
  M'accorda il Prence di vederti.
BEATRICE.
                              Oh Dio!
  Cammillo! . . . oh vista! oh amabil vista! Sei
  Grande davver, se ti sovvien di donna
  Così ravvolta nell' orror.
CAMMILLO.
                        Beatrice!
BEATRICE.
  Misera me! . . . che fu? Ti leggo in volto
  Un affetto turbato.
CAMMILLO.
                    Odi: la fama,
  Che di te per le vie di Roma scorre,
  Mi dà fiero tormento. Ancor non posso
  Crederla vera. Beatrice! i sensi
  Di tenerezza io tutti in te vedea;
  Io crescer ti vedea, spiegar, far bella
  Mostra d'amor filiale, e tutti i raggi
  Della virtù splenderti intorno.
BEATRICE.
                              Ah vuoi
  Morta vedermi di dolor? . . . Io sento
  Divorarmi le viscere . . . Una forza
  Superiore m'invade. Innanzi agli occhi
  Tutto vedo cambiar . . . Cammillo! è vero;
  Ho l'aspetto di rea. Furie tiranne,
  Malvagità, di cui non havvi esempio,
  A' miei danni congiurano. Dovere
  D'anima onesta è l'obliarmi. Io merto
  L'abbandono di tutti, or che son fatta
  Di ribrezzo un oggetto. . . . Ove son io?
  A che rimango in vita! Il perder vita

113

Saria dolce al mio cor; ma onore, fama,
La tua amistà perder, Cammillo, tale
Formerian sul mio cor tetra sciagura
Da vedermi infuriata, risoluta
Gire in traccia d'un ferro, e disperata
Tormi da' vivi anche innocente.

CAMMILLO.

                  Il mio
Cor non si muta, sta' sicura: in breve
Loco avrem di saper. Frattanto ascolta
D'amistà le proteste. I feri modi
Se d'implacabil Giudice non posso
Superare, calmar saprolli in parte:
Saprò con mezzi liberali aprirmi
Strada, ove men potea sperarsi . . . .

BEATRICE.

                E credi
Così me rea?

CAMMILLO.

            Son fuor di me! Il Sovrano
Opre di te m'enumerava dianzi. . . .

BEATRICE.

Dianzi! . . . Signor, non mi parlar di lui . . . .

CAMMILLO.

Come! che fu? Sai, che del padre tuo
Jeri morì da grave età colpito
Aldobrando l'amico? infra i suoi ascosi
Fogli trovar preci di te fervent
Al principe dirette. Dimmi: scritte
Veramente l'hai tu?

BEATRICE.

         Che chiedi!

CAMMILLO.

             Il core
Aprimi tutto. Ogni segreto spiega
Al tuo amico Cammillo. Indi alcun detto
Non temer che si sparga.

114

BEATRICE.

Oh Sventurata!
Piaga mortal dovrò riaprir? Saranno
Scorse otto lune da che scrissi.

CAMMILLO.

Oh cielo!
Fur trattenuti ad arte i fogli. Prima
Di stamani non gli ebbe.

BEATRICE.

Oh ben si vede,
Ch'era Aldobrando di mio padre amico!
Che ti narrava il Principe?

CAMMILLO.

Ah Beatrice!
Quel santo vecchio piangere lo vidi
Sopra i tuoi fogli. Biasimar con voce
Altissima Adldobrando.

BEATRICE.

A te parola
De' miei scritti non tenne?

CAMMILLO.

Ei nol facea;
Ed io chiesto avrei troppo. Alcun non ci ode:
Tua confidenza nel mio sen discenda;
L'amico saldo, vero tuo già pende
Per udir da' tuoi labbri. . . .

BEATRICE.

Oh Dio! a qual passo
Tu sei giunta, o Beatrice! Il gran segreto,
Dopo aver data a me la chiesta calma,
Che dovesse morir credea col prence.
Ma tu fai forza. Come te sublime
Stabile amico non si trova, e merti
Ch'io tutto spieghi. Odimi dunque: io vidi,
Oggi ha il quart'anno, scender nella tomba
La mia tenera madre. La cagione
L'opre del padre furono. Sebbene

115

Foss'io in giovin età, tutto vedea,
Tutto apprendea con gran ribrezzo. Egli era
De' suoi giorni il tiranno. Il reo suo genio
Non si estinse però. L'età mia crebbe
In mezzo alle vergogne. Infami donne
Sovente accanto stavanmi: vedea
Cose, che a dirle l'onestà rifugge,
E non trova parole. Io fatta adulta
Che risolvere: A te mio grande amico
Dirti mai nulla volli: il saggio fugge
Dalla casa degli empj; eri sollievo
Di me tu sol. Che fo? modesta a' piedi
Vo del padre: lo prego a cambiar modi.
E alfin gli dico, che ora venne, in cui
Possan le nozze togliermi. Nemico
Ode più facil di nemico avverso
Peggior proposto. Mi preclude: l'aria
Fino mi toglie, e tor voleami ancora . . . .
Ah Signor, mi perdona! ah mio Cammillo!
Ottimo tu, tu altissimo di sensi
Tu generoso non mi chieder oltre,
Non mi sforzar, che la natura stessa,
La medesma natura onta ne avrebbe.

CAMMILLO.

Ov' è quel cor fermo così, che in pianto
Non si stempri al tuo dire? Ecco ragione
Delle suppliche tue, eccone il fiero
Esito dell'indugio.

BEATRICE.

Al santo vecchio
Chiedea la vita: gli chiedea che tosto
Dalla feroce potestà paterna
Mi togliesse. Ad altrui vil fatta ancella
Mi desse in dono. Ove le vere stanno
Anime tolte dal romor del mondo
Ei mi ponesse; in una tomba peggio
Di rea vestale; mi strappasse in somma
Da quella vita orribile di morte.

CAMMILLO.

      I tuoi martir son miei. Scuopro la grande
      Necessità, che ti spingeva a un passo
      Di virtù, che t'onora; e tutte scopro
      Le funeste vicende, a cui soggetta
      Sta la fama più pura. Ora non bramo
      Udir da te, cosa poi fu, che avvenne
      A quell'uomo feral. Ch'era tuo padre,
      A dispetto di sua mal saggia mente,
      Spero, scordato non avrai: a momenti
      Ti rivedrò: trono al Sovran. . . . ma pria
      Veder Marsilio bramerei . . . .

BEATRICE.

              Mi lasci?
      Mi consoli così?

CAMMILLO.

                Beatrice! è tempo
      Questo prezioso. Tu pur chiama, implora
      Dal coraggio assistenza. La natura,
      Il bisogno di viver, l'evidenza
      Di tua ragion t'alzin lo spirto al sommo,
      Lo rinfranchin; ti rendano all'etade,
      Al sesso, al mondo non oggetto reo,
      Ma di virtude luminoso esempio.

Scena v.

FAUSTO, BEATRICE, CAMMILLO.

FAUSTO.

           Il Giudice s'avanza, o donna . . .

CAMMILLO.

                Or ora . . .

FAUSTO.

      Come tu qui?

CAMMILLO.

            Leggi

(*Presentandogli un foglio.*)

FAUSTO.

Mi prostro al cenno.

CAMMILLO.

Vedere io voglio il Giudice . . .

FAUSTO.

Signore,

Tua guida m'offro.

BEATRICE.

A me ritorna: pensa
Come ne resto.

CAMMILLO.

Non temer: frattanto
L'alma fa' queta. Nobile valore
Vince il destin, vendica l'onte, e pura
Ritorna in seggio l'innocenza oppressa.

Fine dell'Atto Terzo.

ATTO QUARTO.

Scena i.

MARSILIO, FAUSTO.

MARSILIO.

S'appelli Beatrice; e gli altri pure
S'avanzino nell atto . . . Ah Fausto! io temo
Che nero giorno oggi per lor non sia.

FAUSTO.

Bene provvide il Ciel, che colto sempre
Sia da' lacci l'indegno.

MARSILIO, *indi* BEATRICE.

MARSILIO.
                    Ecco la Donna.
Costei da' modi di perfidia affatto
Disgiunta appare. Ma cotanti e tanti
Certi sospetti s'alzano, ferali
Accuse, voci contro d'essa e pianto,
Che rea la fan senza difesa. Saldo
Giudice sto. . . . Siedi donzella. Tolsi
Dall'apparato il pubblico concorso;
Privata causa. . . .
BEATRICE.
                    Come vuoi. Di Roma
Non pavento all'aspetto.
MARSILIO.
                    Almen sostenga
L'innocenza il tuo spirto. Intanto reggi
Al sembiante fatal di chi te rea
Di nera colpa appella.

Scena iii.

FAUSTO *e Soldati, i quali scortano incatenati* MARZIO
e OLIMPIO.
BEATRICE, MARSILIO.

FAUSTO.
                    Ecco al tuo cenno
I malvagi, o Signor.
MARZIO.
                    Che vedo! o Stelle!
Beatrice!
OLIMPIO.
                    Lascia. . . . vo'mirar. . . .

119

MARSILIO.

              Tacete.

La verità sempre sospetta in bocca
De' rei, salvezza dell'onesto or sia.
Tutti sull'orlo per cader ci pose
La comun debolezza. Avventurato
Chi dal dritto sentier non esce, e fassi
Saggio modello agli altri! Il cor sedate
Pria se vi batte; indi ne dite il nome
Primieri voi.

OLIMPIO.

            Risponderò. Noi fummo

Servi già di Franceso: ho nome Olimpio. . . .

MARZIO.

Io Marzio.

MARSILIO.

          Qual stranissima cagione

Vi diè alla fuga?

OLIMPIO.

           Grave rischio.

MARSILIO.

                Chiari

Spiegatevi.

OLIMPIO.

          Il faremo. Il Signor nostro

D'un umore feral, sull'adempito
Dover di servo ben talor solea
Urti e percosse darci. Un viver era
Quello da bruti.

MARSILIO.

         E che! trarvi con altro

Signor non potevate?

OLIMPIO.

          Anzi decisa

Era la nostra voglia.

MARSILIO.

         E chi il disegno

Vi trattenea?

OLIMPIO.

                Beatrice fu. Donzella,
Tu tanto saggia, tu per noi cotanto
Dolce, amorosa scusaci. Comanda
Natura a tutti la difesa.

MARSILIO.

               Espressa
Fate la storia.

OLIMPIO.

              Volentieri. Quando
Noi partir volevamo, ella n'accorse.
Figlia rinchiusa, disperata figlia
Circondata d'affanno, ognor soggetta
A padre iniquo, ove trovarsi freno
Che la ritenga? Diecci un ferro in mano,
Dicendo, mezzo altro non avvi, mezzo
Di questo più sollecito, onde trarci
Dalla comune tirannia.

MARSILIO.

            Beatrice!
Narrano il vero?

BEATRICE.

            Di costoro appena
Mi sovviene.

MARSILIO.

         Tuoi servi essi non furo?

BEATRICE.

    Saranno stati.

MARSILIO.

             Che mai sento! Puoi
Negare tu ciò che sa Roma tutta?

BEATRICE.

    E Roma il sappia; a che conoscer servi
Dovea donzella?

MARSILIO.

        Proseguite.

OLIMPIO.

           Oh noi

Proprio infelici, se la donna segue
A ostinarsi sul ver! Non ci ravvisi?
BEATRICE.
Non mai un leggero sovvenirne esclude
La vostra conoscenza.
OLIMPIO.
                    Il mio coreggio
Comincia a indebolirsi.
MARZIO.
                    Olimpio, bada,
Non ti smarrir. Di noi che fia?
OLIMPIO.
                        Veraci
In tutto siamo. Diecci il ferro. Scesa
Era la notte col silenzio; ed ove
All splendore di facella opaca
Stava dormente di Francesco l'alma,
Inoltrare ci fece. A quella vista
Ella gridò: ferite. . . .
MARSILIO.
                    Il ferro dievvi?
OLIMPIO.
La donna.
MARSILIO.
                Il ferro veggasi.
OLIMPIO.
                    Di colpa
Crudo strumento presso noi serbare
Dovevam forse?
MARSILIO.
                Ecco il pugnale. Attenti
L'esaminate.
MARZIO.
                Ah Olimpio, che dicesti!
Il pugnale era mio, mentir non vuolsi;
Ed affermo che è questo. Io nel presepio
Dove guardian pascea primo i destrieri
Nel vil travaglio l'adoprava.

OLIMPIO.
>   Omai
> L'error chi toglie?

MARSILIO.
>   Quai sommesse voci! . . .
> Tremate, iniqui!

MARZIO.
>   Io parlerò. La morte
> D'evitare non cerco. In me non cade
> Desiderio maligno. Intatta e pura
> La verità vo' dir. D'Olimpio inganno
> Fu l'asserir che la donzella in mano
> Cel recassè.

MARSILIO.
>   Perfidia invan si cela.
> Reo principio! Seguite.

OLIMPIO.
>   Eccomi . . . .

MARZIO.
>   Olimpio,
> Lascia ch'io narri; veggo chiaro il fatto . . . .

OLIMPIO.
> Anch'io; non dubitare. A quell'aspetto,
> Dell'assopito signor nostro in core
> Pietà ci prese. Ei così solo e inerme;
> Noi forti e armati, in quello stato darlo
> Non volevamo in modo niuno a morte.

MARSILIO.
> E perchè il deste?

OLIMPIO.
>   La donzella ardita
> Ci tolse il ferro dalle mani, e piena
> D'un furor tanto reo, quanto improvviso,
> Al letto corse per ferir, gridando
> Spirto apprender da femmina dovrete!
> Tale rampogna ci passò nel core,
> Furie crude movendo: e così fatti
> Dal suo desìo più che dal nostro fieri,

Con tre mortali pugnalate l'alma
Gli togliemmo dal petto; e la donzella
Tuttor furente a me di nuovo il ferro
Rapì di mano, e sopra il corpo spento
Vibrava un colpo.

MARSILIO.

      Osservisi Franceso
(Prende dei folgi, e legge.)
Morì trafitto da tre colpi. Il quarto
Non v'era.

MARZIO.

      A me lascia parlar. Tu bene
Come andò non rammenti. All'opra mano
Non pose Beatrice.

MARSILIO.

      Ah traditori!
Così la mente del feral misfatto
Piena tenete? ove sarà chi apprenda
Qual sia il vero da voi? chi riconosca
L'innocenza o il delitto? Ebben, tu a cui
Par che memoria meglio assista, e in pregio
L'onesto sia, segui a narrar.

MARZIO.

      Nel petto
Timor mi scende . . . ma coraggio . . . ah invano
Lo cerco in me! . . . quivi d'averlo è forza . . .

MARSILIO.

Tremi? . . .

MARZIO.

      No, no: sol nel racconto Olimpio
Fallò, qual dissi. . . .

MARSILIO.

      Non m'inganno. Al certo
Tu di lui sei più reo; ma ti tradisce
Lo spavento dell'alma.

MARZIO.

      Ah no! deh lascia
Ch'io tutto dica: verità paleso.

Beatrice poi che dell'oprar malvagio
Colpevoli ci rese, e a un tempo ardita
Seppe mostrarsi e snaturata figlia;
L'estinto corpo, onde coprire il fero
Suo attentato nefando, a noi commise
Che dal balcon . . . dove una balza scende. . . .
Oh lasso me! non ho più spirto . . . , voce
E cor mi trema. . . .

MARSILIO.
     Empj! così tentaste
Scemar la colpa?

MARZIO.
     Son perduto . . . Olimpio,
Prosegui tu, non t'avvilire. . . .

OLIMPIO.
    Fredda
Tema ho nel sen: non veggo scampo.

MARZIO.
      Scampo
Questo manto ci dia. Lo vedi?

BEATRICE.
      Il veggo.

MARSILIO.
Di chi fu questo manto?

MARZIO.
     Alla donzella
Il chiedi.

BEATRICE.
     Un manto di mio padre egli era. . . .

MARSILIO.
Chi a voi lo dià?

MARZIO.
     Beatrice il diede. Puoi
Negarlo tu? come acquistarlo, come
Senza di te?

BEATRICE.
     Ve' scellerati! forse
A chi la vita al padre mio togliea

125

Con tanta arte e furor, difficil era
Togliergli un manto?
MARZIO.
                    Più non reggo. Il suolo
Veggo girare. Mi ha tradito il core. . . .
Sento di morte i palpiti.
OLIMPIO.
                    La mente
Più non mi regge. . . . Marzio . . . .
MARZIO.
                    Se difesa
Più a noi non resta, di salvare almeno
Tentiam Beatrice.
MARSILIO.
                    I perfidi capaci
Fur di rimorso alfin. Che dite? Strada
Altra vi resta? Più di voi confuso
Scellerato chi vide?
MARZIO.
                    E chi non giunse
La giustizia del cielo! il ver trionfa.
Signore or chiara ti farem nostr' alma:
Disperazione, odio crudel, desìo
Di vendetta, che in cor de' servi è forte,
Ci spinsero al misfatto. Era Francesco
Così feroce di maniere e strano
Colla sua gente, che null'altro mai
Speri agguagliarlo. Si di male in male
Passavamo i dì nostri allor che fera
Voglia ci armò la scellerata mano
Contra l'empio signor. Spento costui,
Ci pensammo felici. Era Beatrice
L'idolo nostro; il suo bel cor, la schietta
Virtude sua, l'eccelsa anima grande
Ci promettevan taciti ogni bene.
Ma non ha ben la colpa: il cielo è giusto.
Consumato il terribile misfatto
Avammo appena, che i rimorsi crudi
E il timor ci angustiavano. Dovunque

126

Scritta di noi l'orribile sentenza
Vedevamo; e che ognun sapesse il nostro
Delitto temevamo. In questa orrenda
Atroce lotta di continua pena
Di lasciar risolvemmo quelle mura,
Dove il sangue tuttor stava rappreso,
Quel sangue, che versammo . . . oh Dio! eseguite
Sopra di noi fero comando. A iniqui
Non risparmiate la condegna morte.

OLIMPIO.
Ve la chiediamo, l'imploriamo; a noi
Fatta è la vita insopportabil peso.

MARSILIO.
Ite: il destino, che v'aspetta udrete
(Marzio e Olimpio vengono tradotti altrove.)
Libera sei donzella. Il fausto evento
Or sappia Roma. Libertà s'accordi
Tosto a' suoi servi.
             (Si ritira con Fausto e i soldati.)

Scena iv.

CAMMILLO, BEATRICE.

CAMMILLO.
             E sarà ver, Beatrice,
Che innocente al mio sen ti stringa? oh come
Tutto a un tratto variò! . . . Che fù? il sembiante
Lieto non mostri.

BEATRICE.
             Oh mio Cammillo! Ho il core
Assediato così da tanti affetti.
Che fuor di me quasi mi rendon.

CAMMILLO.
                      Grande
È la prova, ch'hai data. Omai conviene
La rimembranza infin toglier dal petto
Degli acerbi infortunj.

127

BEATRICE.
>   Ah s'allontana
> Da me la pace. La tristezza accanto
> Eterna mi si pone.

CAMMILLO.
>   O Beatrice!
> Nulla avrei fatto, se da queste mura
> Torre non ti sapessi. Il cor disponi
> A lasciare di Roma il tetro aspetto,
> Ove per te stanno memorie vive
> Di tanto lutto. Andiam dell' Arno in riva;
> Là dove il ciel tanto propizio splende
> Sopra l'arti, e le scienze. Andiamo dove
> L'Adige e il Pò fecondano l'amene
> Ubertose campagne. Varcheremo
> Le gelid'Alpi, e le profonde valli,
> Che il Rodano divide. Il mar vedremo
> Ibero quindi, noi vedrem la Senna,
> E tutto ciò che più vorrai. Ti prego
> Al mio desìo d'esser concorde. Parlo
> Coll'esperienza a lato. Il tetro umore,
> Che in me produsse d'Eleonora il fato.
> D'Eleonora mia tanto amata moglie,
> Spariva a vista degli strani lidi,
> Che a te narrava.

BEATRICE.
>   Una feroce larva
> Incatenati tienmi i piedi e il core:
> Di Roma escire non poss'io.

CAMMILLO.
>   Che dici!
> Vo'sollevarti.

BEATRICE.
>   Un impossibil chiedi:
> È volere del ciel ch'io viva in pianto.

Fine dell'Atto Quarto.

ATTO QUINTO.

Scena i.

BEATRICE, FAUSTO.

FAUSTO.

> Gli empj a te chiedon di parlar. Donzella,
> Sorda mostrarsi all domanda fora
> Laudabil opra. Pensa tu al delitto
> Onde son rei. Davanti a te maligno
> Desìo gli spinge, e cercano all pena
> Disperato riparo. Con eccessi
> D'una coscienza tormentata immenso
> Sfogheranno, vedrai. Dolor mentito,
> Si disciorranno in lagrime per trarti
> Al biasimevol passo, onde clemenza
> Loro implorar tu debba. Ormai costante
> È la voglia del Giudice, che a morte
> Ambo li danna.

BEATRICE.

>   Il so so ancor che han gli empj
> I loro privilegi. È ver che figlia,
> A cui da lor barbaramente spento
> Fu il padre, non dovria cedere a'prieghi,
> Non dovrebbe sentire in cor pietade.
> Ma se pensiam che un breve istante è quello,
> Che prudenza e ragion può torre al saggio,
> Saprem del reo, non già scemar la pena,
> Tollerar la presenza. Le passioni
> Date ci fur dal ciel per vita nostra,
> E per nostro tormento. Ha dritto ognora
> D'esser udito il reo. Fa'che in privato
> Modo tosto s'inoltrino.

Scena ii.

BEATRICE.

Noi siamo
Senza saper chi siamo. . . . Oh di natura
Profondissimo arcano, che ci pone
Nella speranza, nel timore, e mai
Giorno non torna, che non dia vigore
Alla speme e alla tema! . . . Eccoli. Io sono
Nella più tetra circostanza, in cui
Possa condurre orribile fortuna.

Scena iii.

MARZIO, OLIMPIO *semplicemente incatenati*, BEATRICE.

BEATRICE.
Che volete?
MARZIO.

Sentenza a noi di sangue
Fu pronunciata. Ci sarià la morte,
Donzella, intollerabile, se prima
A te d'esporre non ci fosse dato
Le nostre voglie e i mali.
BEATRICE.

Io v'odo.
MARZIO.

Ormai
Moriam, donzella; non v'ha speme. Almeno
Con intrepido cor moriamo entrambi,
Poichè te salva il morir nostro. In faccia
Non ci restano giudici. Dell'alma
Possiamo espor liberamente i sensi.
Segreta morte ebbe tuo padre, ed era
Degno di averla pubblica, nefanda,
Se povero nascea. Sovente al grande
Accordare vediam ciò che ad uom vile

130

Negato viene . . . mai! parlar di cose
Inutili a che serve? Amata madre,
Che curva sta sull'ottantesimo anno,
Lascio, Beatrice. Dalla mia partita,
Che oggi scorreva la primiera luna,
Nuova di lei non seppi. Circondata
La tanto buona sventurata vecchia
Sarà dalla miseria. Io la campava
Cogli avanzi, che trar sapea da questa
Generosa magione. In mezzo al pianto,
Se mai vive tuttor, sarà infelice
Per cagion di mia fuga. La consola;
Tu che siei tanto liberale, e pronta
A sollevare chi infelice vive,
Falle arrivar qualche soccorso. Almeno
Se il cielo ancor viva la vuol, lo stento
Soccomber non la faccia.
BEATRICE.
                    Ha nome!
Nell'asciugarsi con un fazzoletto gli occhi.)
MARZIO.
                    Fabia.
BEATRICE.
    La conosce Lorenzo?
MARZIO.
                    Al certo.
BEATRICE.
                    Chiedi
    Nulla tu?
OLIMPIO.
            Beatrice! di parenti
    Vedovo affatto mi ritrovo. Io voglio
    Proprio per te spender mia vita, senza
    Il menomo guadagno.
BEATRICE.
            Ma placati
    D'animo state: non morrete.
MARZIO.
            Come! . . .

131

Senti, o donzella. L'opera migliore,
Che aspettar l'universo da noi possa,
Da noi vil gente, non mai pianta, e sempre
Infra lo spregio, è la spontanea morte.
OLIMPIO.
Siam risoluti; siamo fermi; siamo
Veramente tranquilli.
BEATRICE.
                              Ite: frappoco
Cosa di me udirete.

    (Si ritirano.)

                Scena iv.

        FAUSTO, BEATRICE.

FAUSTO.
                              I Servi tutti
Voglion vederti, o Beatrice.
BEATRICE.
                              Alcuno
Fa' che non resti . . . . *(I servi d'ogni sesso
          s'avanzano.)* Oh buona gente! oh quanto
Duolmi d'averti disturbata.

    Gli Uomini.
            Ah prendi! . . .
Sacrato a te sia d'allegrezza immensa
Il pianto che versiamo.

    Le Donne.
          A nuova vita
Siam ritornate. . . .
BEATRICE.
          Alla futura vostra
Fortuna voglio provveder. Lorenzo!

N'abbia ciascun perpetuo pane; e perda
La qualità, se vuol, di servo.

    Gli Uomini.
        Oh Dio!
Che mai dici, donzella! infin che spirto
Avremo noi, sacrati a te noi siamo.

    Le Donne.
Non ci dar questa pena. A che la vita
Senza di te?
BEATRICE.
        Non proseguite: il core
L'ho in un lago di pianto. Odi: pur n'abbia
Fabia, di Marzio sconsolata madre,
Generosa assistenza. . . . Oh mia Teresa!
Tu resterai. Voi rivedrò *(Partono i servi facendo
    segni del più estremo dolore.)*: mi reca
Nappo d'onda purissima. Sollievo
Darà al cor fiacco *(Teresa eseguisce l'ordine.)*
        Viver io! macchiata
Nel dolce april così degli anni? . . . Idee
Non ho precise; la confusa mente
Riflessione non piega. . . . E questo è il seno
Dove riposte le virtudi sono? . . .
In me virtude? *(Torna Teresa col bicchiere pieno
    d'acqua.)* . . . Lascialo. . . . Teresa!
Dammi un amplesso. Tiemmi in cor . . . tua rara
Fedeltà riconobbi. Moderata
Più non sarà la tua fortuna. . . . oh Dio!
A che l'affanno? . . . Il volto allegra! Tutti
Dobbiam sparir. Ritirati. . . . *(Parte Teresa piangendo
    dirottamente.)*   Chi para
L'onor, che fugge! Chi l'orror, l'infamia,
Che s'avanzan veloci? . . . ecco il gran mezzo.
    (Trae fuori una piccola cartuccia.)
Tremate, o Padri, se il dover su i figli
Non adempite intero. . . . *(Versa nel bicchiere il veleno,*

che serà dentro la detta cartuccia.)
Ecco qual prole
N'arriva *(Beve.)* ... Ahimè! più non vivrò fra un'ora. ...
Non tremarmi alma rea! Tempo pur giunse
Di verità ... Che fu?

Scena v.

IPPOLITO, BEATRICE.

IPPOLITO.
Beatrice, io sono
Fuor di me dal piacer.
BEATRICE.
Tenero Amico!
Eccone alfine il desiato e tanto
Sospirato momento. ...
IPPOLITO.
Il cor mi balza! ...
Oh me felice! e sarà ver?
BEATRICE.
Lorenzo!
(Lorenzo esce.)
Vo' parlare a Marsilio.

Scena vi.

MARSILIO, BEATRICE, IPPOLITO, *indi* CAMMILLO.

MARSILIO.
Pria del cenno
Ver te movea.
CAMMILLO.
Beatrice! il santo Vecchio
Teco s'allegra, e libertà n'accorda
D'abbandonar le patrie afflitte mura.

Altro a te non riman, che sul momento
Di balzar sopra l'asse: è tutto in pronto.
Teresa tua venga e Lorenzo. Io spero
Vederti lieta sotto un nuovo cielo.

BEATRICE.

Ben altra voglia è fissa in me . . . Cammillo!

CAMMILLO.

Mi sorprende tua voce.

BEATRICE.

Deh! non voglio
In odio al ver star sempre, n'ascoltate
Alfin parole di ribrezzo estremo.
Prima, Signor, commuta a' rei la pena. . . .

MARSILIO.

Che dici mai!

BEATRICE.

Cotanto rei non sono,
Quanto si fanno i miseri. Non era
In lor desìo di toglier vita al padre.

MARSILIO.

E di chi fu?

BEATRICE.

Che mai ricerchi? . . . lascia
Che sempre possa nell'eterno oblio
Restar sepolto il caso.

MARSILIO.

Ma giustizia . . . .

BEATRICE.

Cosa è giustizia! . . . Che facea giustizia
Sull'operar d'un perfido? . . . ah che dico!
Era mio padre; non mi diè alla vita?
Son io la rea. . . . Perdono! Un cuor che è pieno
Tanto di duol, trabocca.

CAMMILLO.

Non la intendo. . . .

IPPOLITO.

Misero me!

MARSILIO.

Spiegati.

135

BEATRICE.

Si, giustizia

Non vedremo oltraggiata. All'ara innanzi
Vedrà cader vittima tal contrita. . . .

CAMMILLO.

Tu vaneggi, o Beatrice. . . . Ama i tuoi giorni . . .

BEATRICE.

Non posso . . . oh Dio! Vita può render scema
La cagion di mie lacrime? ho perduto
Ogni dritto alla vita. Non mi resta
Che il soccorso del ciel. Natura invece
Di produr sulla terra una mia pari
Meglio saria, meglio saria che stesse
Venti lustri infeconda.

CAMMILLO.

Eh sorgi! . . .

IPPOLITO.

T'alza

Dal tuo delirio!

CAMMILLO.

Le paterne mura

Il sen t'ingombran di pensier funesti. . . .
Ti fan pensar cose crudeli.

BEATRICE.

Ho l'alma

Abbattuta così, che più non veggo
Chiari gli oggetti.

CAMMILLO.

Son disposto. Io voglio

Di tutto in onta toglierti. . . .

BEATRICE.

Ma dove

Potrei mostrarmi io disperata donna
Da rapir sino a' fiori il grato odore,
Da intorbidare le più limpid' onde,
Da avvelenar quell' aria ove respiri?
Son fuor di me. . . . Teresa! accorri *(Esce Teresa,
la quale accorre, e la sorregge.)* . . . Il Sole

Stamane alzossi nero sì, ma notte
Tremenda più scende coll'ira e il sangue. . . .
Vendica la natura . . . .

CAMMILLO.
                    E chi resiste
All scena feral? . . .

IPPOLITO.
                    Tosco possente
Prese certo Beatrice. . . . è questo il nappo . . . .
Nero fondo mirate!

MARSILIO.
                    Ecco palese
La vera colpa.

BEATRICE.
                        Oh figli, dal mio esempio . . .
Qualunque atroce paternale offesa
Imparate a soffrir . . . voi padri . . . ah basta! . . .
Servitù grave chi può dar che agguagli
Quella del padre mio? Lieto sembiante
Mostra il cielo . . . si fa più l'aria bella. . . .
Chi il crederia? . . . fino l'informe massa . . . .
Tutto il creato di mia morte gode.

FINE.

Scripta humanistica

Published Volumes

1. Everett W. Hesse, *The "Comedia" and Points of View.* $24.50.
2. Marta Ana Diz, *Patronio y Lucanor: la lectura inteligente "en el tiempo que es turbio."* Prólogo de John Esten Keller. $26.00.
3. James F. Jones, Jr., *The Story of a Fair Greek of Yesteryear.* A Translation from the French of Antoine-François Prévost's *L'Histoire d'une Grecque moderne.* With Introduction and Selected Bibliography. $30.00.
4. Colette H. Winn, *Jean de Sponde: Les sonnets de la mort ou La Poétique de l'accoutumance.* Préface par Frédéric Deloffre. $22.50.
5. Jack Weiner, *"En busca de la justicia social: estudio sobre el teatro español del Siglo de oro."* $24.50.
6. Paul A. Gaeng, *Collapse and Reorganization of the Latin Nominal Flection as Reflected in Epigraphic Sources.* Written with the assistance of Jeffrey T. Chamberlin. $24.00.
7. Edna Aizenberg, *The Aleph Weaver: Biblical, Kabbalistic, and Judaic Elements in Borges.* $25.00.
8. Michael G. Paulson and Tamara Alvarez-Detrell, *Cervantes, Hardy, and "La fuerza de la sangre."* $25.50.
9. Rouben Charles Cholakian, *Deflection/Reflection in the Lyric Poetry of Charles d'Orléans: A Psychosemiotic Reading.* $25.00.

10. Kent P. Ljungquist, *The Grand and the Fair: Poe's Landscape Aesthetics and Pictorial Techniques.* $27.50.

11. D. W. McPheeters, *Estudios humanísticos sobre la "Celestina."* $20.00.

12. Vittorio Felaco, *The Poetry and Selected Prose of Camillo Sbarbaro.* Edited and Translated by Vittorio Felaco. With a Preface by Franco Fido. $25.00.

13. María del C. Candau de Cavallos, *Historia de la lengua española.* $33.00.

14. *Renaissance and Golden Age Studies in Honor of D. W. McPheeters.* Ed. Bruno M. Damiani. $25.00.

15. Bernardo Antonio González, *Parábolas de identidad: Realidad interior y estrategia narrativa en tres novelistas de postguerra* $28.00

16. Carmelo Gariano, *La Edad Media (Aproximación Alfonsina).* $30.00

17. Gabriella Ibieta, *Tradition and Renewal in "La gloria de don Ramiro"* $27.50

18. *Estudios literarios en honor de Gustavo Correa.* Eds. Manuel Durán, Charles Faulhaber, Richard Kinkade, T. A. Perry. $25.00.

19. George Yost, *Pieracci and Shelley: An Italian Ur-Cenci.* $24.00.

Forthcoming

* Carlo Di Maio, *Antifeminism in Selected Works of Enrique Jardiel Poncela.* $20.50.

* Philip J. Spartano, *Giacomo Zanella: Poet, Essayist, and Critic of the "Risorgimento."* Preface by Roberto Severino. $24.00.

* Juan de Mena, *Coplas de los siete pecados mortales: Second and Third Continuations.* Ed. Gladys Rivera. $25.50.

* Barbara Mujica, *Spanish Pastoral Characters.* $25.00.

* Susana Hernández Araico, *La ironía en tragedias de Calderón.* $25.00.

* Francisco Delicado, *Portrait of Lozana: The Exuberant Andalusian Woman*. Translation, introduction and notes by Bruno M. Damiani. $33.00.
* Salvatore Calomino, *From Verse to Prose: The Barlaam and Josaphat Legend in Fifteenth-Century Germany*. $28.00.
* Darlene Lorenz-González, *A Phonemic Description of the Andalusian Dialect Spoken in Almogía, Málaga - Spain*. $25.00.
* Juan de Mena, *Coplas de los siete pecados mortales: Second and Third Continuation*. Ed. Gladys Rivera. $25.50.
* Maricel Presilla, *The Politics of Death in the "Cantigas de Santa María."* $27.50.
* Zelda I. Brooks, *The Poetry of Gabriel Celaya*. $26.00
* Jorge Checa, *Gracián y la imaginación arquitectónica* $28.00